The Power
of Patience

The Power of Patience

How to Slow the Rush and Enjoy More Happiness,
Success, and Peace of Mind Every Day

M. J. Ryan

MJF BOOKS
NEW YORK

Published by MJF Books
Fine Communications
322 Eighth Avenue
New York, NY 10001

The Power of Patience
LC Control Number: 2009932335
ISBN-13: 978-1-56731-985-9
ISBN-10: 1-56731-985-8

This edition is published by MJF Books by arrangement with Broadway Books,
an imprint of The Crown Publishing Group, a division of Random House, Inc.

Printed in the United States of America.

MJF Books and the MJF colophon are trademarks of Fine Creative Media, Inc.

QF 10 9 8 7 6

The key to everything is patience.
You get the chicken by hatching
the egg, not smashing it.

Arnold H. Glasgow

Contents

The Power
of Patience

1.

HOW THIS OLD-FASHIONED
VIRTUE CAN IMPROVE
YOUR LIFE

Dear God,
I pray for patience.
And I want it RIGHT NOW!

Oren Arnold

Consider this:

❋ Some McDonald's are promising lunch in ninety seconds or it's free.

❋ The average doctor visit now lasts eight minutes.

❋ An over-the-counter drug is marketed for women who "don't have time for a yeast infection."

❋ Politicians currently take a mere 8.2 seconds to answer a question, regardless of the complexity of the topic.

❋ A popular all-you-can-eat buffet in Tokyo charges by the minute—the faster you eat, the cheaper it is.

❈ Kodak is launching one-hour film development shops at Disney World, in hotel lobbies, and in amusement parks so you can have your pictures before the vacation is over.

❈ The head of Hitachi's portable computer division motivates his workers with the slogan: "Speed is God, and time is the devil."

❈ Developers of high rises have discovered an upward limit to the number of floors—the amount of time people are willing to wait for elevators. Fifteen seconds is what feels best; if it stretches to forty, we freak out.

All of us these days, it seems, spend our lives rushing around. We're in constant motion, and we expect everything and everyone around us to go faster as well. As technology watcher David Shenk notes, between our modems and our speed dials, faxes, beepers, and FedEx, "quickness has disappeared from our culture. We now only experience degrees of slowness." Writer James Gleick says it more bluntly—we're all suffering from "hurry sickness," a term first coined by Meyer Friedman, the identifier of the Type A personality.

I know I have it. I can't stand how slowly my computer boots up. I actually timed it recently; it took two minutes and I was fidgeting the whole time. I'm the person pushing the elevator button more than once to make it come faster. I hit the pound key to bypass the message on other people's voice mail. And I use the one-minute button on the microwave because it's quicker than punching in the time myself.

This is how bad I've got it. Yesterday, I went to my local copy shop. I made my copies and was standing in line, waiting to pay. The young man behind the counter was struggling to help a very old lady figure out how to send a package to her grandchild. There's one other person in line in front of me. My inner monologue goes like this: Lines, I hate lines. Why can't they get enough help in here? (Fume.) Why can't they at least post how much they charge for copies so I could pay without waiting? (A minute passes. More fuming.) I don't have time for this. I've got more important things to do. I can't just stand here. I have to get home and write this book on patience.

I can't take it anymore. I blurt out from my place in line, "How much for a copy?" "Ten cents," replies the flustered young man. Flinging down a dollar for my forty-cent purchase, I storm out of the store, the irony of the situation not occurring to me until I am driving away.

Another word for hurry sickness is impatience, and I'm pretty sure I'm not the only one suffering from it. Road rage, violence of all sorts, blowups at the office, divorce, yelling at our kids . . . all of these and many other of the world's ills can be traced at least in part to a lack of patience.

Recently the state of California has been running public service announcements to "slow for the cone zone." It's a campaign to get drivers to slow from sixty-five to fifty-five miles per hour in construction areas because so many workers have been killed. The ads inform listeners that the time difference between going fifty-five and sixty-five in a one-mile construction area is ten seconds. People are getting killed because we're not willing to get somewhere ten-seconds-a-mile later!

Indeed it appears that the faster things go, the less patience we are able to muster. This is a problem because life inevitably has a certain degree of delay in the form of lines, traffic jams, and automated message systems. More important, our lack of patience creates difficulties because the more complex of life's challenges—illness, disability, relationship conflicts, job crises, parenting issues, to name a few—require that we practice patience in order not merely to cope, but to grow in love and wisdom.

Without patience, we can't truly learn from the lessons life throws at us; we're unable to mature. We remain at the stage of irritable babies, unable to delay gratification more than momentarily, unable to work toward what we truly want in any dedicated way. If we want to live wider and deeper lives, not just faster ones, we have to practice patience—patience with ourselves, with other people, and with the big and small circumstances of life itself.

I know we're longing to put more patience in our lives because I've published over two hundred books and written twenty-two. Never before had people said to me so emphatically, "I need that!" when I told them what I was working on. But with this book, every person who heard of it said something to that effect. The world is going faster and faster and we are all trying to keep up. Never before has patience been more needed—and never has it been in such short supply.

But we can change that. With the right attitudes and a bit of practice, we can learn to harness the power of patience in our lives. If I, a speeded-up, Type A, overachieving middle-aged woman can do it, so can you. It's a combination of motivation (wanting to), awareness (paying attention to our inner landscape), and cultivation (practicing).

We can do it because patience is a human quality that can be strengthened. We have what we need. We're patient already—how else did we get through school, learn to love, find a job? We're just not always aware of what helps us be patient, what triggers our impatience, or what to do when our patience wears thin.

The most important thing to know is that patience is something you *do*, not something you have or don't have. It's like a muscle. We all have muscles, but some people are stronger than others because they work out.

The same is true with patience. Some of us may be better at it right now, but each of us can develop more with practice. That's what this book is all about.

The Power of Patience looks at the importance of patience— what it can do for us, why it's so crucial now, and how to become more patient. It does this from a broad spiritual and inspirational point of view, using my own stories as well as ideas from centuries of wisdom on the topic from around the world. It springs from my quest to live a happy and meaningful life, and my passion to help others do the same.

This has been a lifelong search for me, but it began to take shape about ten years ago, when I, as the executive editor of Conari Press, put together a little book with some friends called *Random Acts of Kindness*. It seemed like a good idea at the time—let's do nice little things for strangers—but when I began to see and hear about the effects it was having, I began to sense I had stumbled onto something very important. Suddenly I was inundated with letters from people telling me of the joy they had experienced as either a doer or a receiver of these acts. The letter I will never forget was from a high school student who said he was going to kill himself, until he read our book and decided that maybe life was worth living.

I became fascinated with the power of kindness to create happiness, and went on to help write a series of books on the topic. And I began to try to become more kind, both to strangers and those I am close to. And lo and behold, just like the boy who didn't kill himself, I got happier.

Then I began to wonder, If kindness can have such a positive effect, what other qualities right under our noses could have similar results? I turned my attention to gratitude, and discovered that the more I cultivated a sense of appreciation for all that I had, the happier and less fearful I was. Again, I wrote about my experiences, this time in *Attitudes of Gratitude*, which also seemed to strike a chord. And once again, I received many letters, this time about the power of gratitude.

My study of gratitude, the awareness of all that we are receiving, led me naturally to generosity, the giving of ourselves and our resources to someone else, in *The Giving Heart*, which then led me, naturally, to patience. For the more we cultivate patience, the happier and more peaceful we are, even if things don't always turn out the way we want.

Using a bit more patience, I could have waited calmly for the (maybe) five minutes it would have taken to pay at the copy shop. I would not have had those negative feelings of irritation and anger, and I would not have upset the other people in the store. My blood pressure would have remained low, my immune system strong. I would have been more content—even while waiting!

Indeed, the longer I study and practice patience, the more I've come to see that it is a crucial factor in whether we have satisfying lives or not. Patience gives us self-control, the capacity to stop and be in the present moment. From that place we can make wise choices. Patience helps us be more loving toward others, more at ease with the circumstances of our lives, and more able to get what we want. It constantly rewards us with the fruits of maturity and wisdom: healthier relationships, higher-quality work, and peace of mind. It accomplishes this magic by bringing together three essential qualities of mind and heart that allow us to be and do our best: persistence, serenity, and acceptance.

STICK-TO-IT-NESS: THE POWER OF PERSISTENCE

Patience gives us stick-to-it-ness, the ability to work steadily toward our goals and dreams. Recent research in emotional intelligence demonstrates that the effect of such persistence can equal many IQ points. Asian students in the United States are thought to be, on average, within one or two IQ points of Caucasians. But because they are usually taught persistence when young, they end up, as a group, behaving as though they have a much higher average IQ and are disproportionately represented in top universities and highly intellectual professions.

I once read an interview with the founder of *Fast Company* magazine, one of the few dot-com–related media still standing after the dot bust. He had had an idea to create a magazine that reflected the new ideas of the times and he pursued it despite huge obstacles. He borrowed against his personal credit cards and stormed the country, trying to get investors. No takers. But he passionately believed in his idea and refused to give up. Literally the day he was down to his last dime and had run out of options, he made the connection that led to the founding of the magazine—

and ultimately to his selling it to a publishing conglomerate for a huge sum.

Stories abound about folks who persisted despite the odds, before finally achieving great success. Walt Disney, for instance, was turned down 302 times before he got financing for Disneyland. George Lucas put up his own money to make *Star Wars* because no one believed in his vision. By the time the movie came out, he was completely broke. But he ended up becoming phenomenally wealthy precisely because he had been unable to sell any of the rights to the film or sequels.

Patiently continuing on despite obstacles doesn't mean that we will necessarily reap the kind of huge reward Mr. Fast Company, Walt Disney, or George Lucas did. But it sure increases the odds that we will make our own personal dreams come true, whatever they are.

NO REASON TO STRESS:
THE POWER OF SERENITY

Patience also gives us calmness of spirit. With patience, our inner experience is more like a still pond than a raging river. Rather than being thrown into anger, panic, or fear by every circumstance life throws at us—a canceled plane, a missed deadline by a workmate, our spouse forgetting to do an errand—we are able to put it into some kind of perspective that allows us to keep our cool.

With this composure, rather than being the miserable kvetch

who upsets everyone around us, we're the ones people look to for comfort and humor when things go awry. Jesuit priest and author Anthony de Mello describes this attitude when he writes, "All is well, all is well. Though everything is a mess, all is well."

With patience, we are more able to stay calm on the inside no matter what is happening on the outside. We trust in our capacity to deal with whatever comes our way. And that trust gives great peace of mind.

One reason for this is that a synonym for patience is self-possession. I love that word; it helps me remember that, with patience, we are in charge of our selves. We can choose how to respond to a given event, rather than being hijacked by our emotions. In this way, patience is like a keel on a boat—it allows us to keep our stability in the stormiest of seas while continuing to move in the direction we desire.

THAT'S OK: THE POWER
OF ACCEPTANCE

Patience also gives us the ability to put up graciously with obstacles in our path, to respond to life's challenges with courage, strength, and optimism. A business failure, disappointments in love, a serious disability, money woes—these are just a few of the trials that we might be faced with over the course of a lifetime. Being patient in these circumstances doesn't mean that we have to like the curve-balls that get hurled at us. But we recognize that they come with being alive and so we don't add the additional suffering of bitterness, revenge, or hopelessness to the mix. Rather than whining or complaining, we roll up our sleeves and tackle the task at hand.

Patience in the form of acceptance also allows us to have empathy for others, because we recognize that as human beings, we all have limitations. It gives us the emotional resilience to respond with kindness, to feel compassion.

When you lovingly tend to an elderly parent who never thanks you, when you calmly explain to a fussy two-year-old for the forty-seventh time why he can't climb on the furniture, you are demonstrating patience, putting up with situations that given your preference you'd rather not, because you understand they are created by people who are, like you, flawed human beings who just want to be happy.

Through this acceptance of others as they are, and of life as it is showing up right now, we prove our true strength and beauty as human beings. It's easy to be accepting when all is well. But when we are patient when things aren't going the way we want, we truly shine as heroes.

Take a moment to reflect on a time when you employed the power of patience. What were the circumstances? Did you calm an otherwise volatile situation? Treat someone you care about better than if you had blown your stack? How did it feel? What helped you to act patiently? What happened as a result?

Now think about a time when someone was patient with you. How did he or she treat you? How did it feel? What were you able to do or learn as a consequence?

It is because patience is so valuable that all religions offer us models to follow. Buddhists are taught that practicing the patience of the Buddha is one of the ways to reach enlightenment, while patience is one of the ninety-nine divine attributes of God in the Koran. In the Old Testament, Job is the epitome of patience, while Christians are inspired by the life and sacrifice of Jesus Christ.

Because of the value of patience, I have no doubt that at one time or other, someone has told you that you "should" be more patient. Perhaps that's how you talk to yourself or your kids. (I know I do.) Did it work? Most likely not. Merely telling ourselves we should do something—and then beating ourselves up when we don't—is not effective. All it does is create blame and shame.

Impatience is a habit; so is patience. To change a habit, we need strong motivation, which comes from knowing the rewards that come from the new behavior. That's why this book begins with a look at Patience's Gifts. Next, we need a mindset that encourages the change we want to see. The Attitudes of Patience chapter presents the mental outlooks that strengthen the habit. Finally we need the tools of change. We need to experiment with new behaviors and notice the effects they have in our lives. In the section titled The Practices of Patience, you'll discover a number of ways to cultivate this habit of the heart, particularly in the ordinary stressful situations you find yourself in—things like standing in line, taking care of kids, dealing with aging parents, crawling in traffic jams, waiting on hold, waiting for love.

This book is meant to be read slowly, to be fully felt and lived with. As you practice, I encourage you not to feel you must do every suggestion—that will stand in your way of doing any. Start by trying one or two that you feel drawn to. I offer a lot of ideas because I don't know which will be most effective for you.

This is soul work as well as mind training and it takes practice and time. I have been consciously practicing patience for several years now and there are still occasions when I blow my stack.

You'll hear about those times and what I'm still learning, for I don't hold myself out as an expert. Think of me rather as a fellow traveler on the journey. In these pages, I offer you my hand as we explore ways, through patience, that we can become more grounded and less overwhelmed, more powerful and loving, and more effective with all those who cross our path.

This is exciting work, because it promises to help us reclaim our time, our priorities, and our ability to respond to life and all of its demands. With patience, we are in the driver's seat of our own lives. Patience plants us firmly in the ground of our being, content with who and where we are. Patience makes us happier, it leads us to success, and it gives us greater peace of mind every day. Who could resist that invitation?

It is my hope and prayer that this book will help you grow the patience that is in your heart, and that your efforts and mine will ripple out into the world to create a tidal wave. For if we as a community of human souls harness the power of patience, there is no problem we can't solve—eventually.

2.

PATIENCE'S GIFTS

If there is anything that gives kingliness to the soul, it is patience.
What was the secret of the masters who have accomplished
great things, who have inspired many and who have
helped many souls? Their secret was patience.

Inayat Khan

Before we begin to learn anything, we always want to know why we
should bother. It's not a cynical question, but springs from genuine
curiosity. Learning anything takes desire, so we have to know why
it's worth the effort to put in the required energy. That's why we
begin by looking at what we'll get for our efforts, the rewards of becoming more patient.

PATIENCE CREATES EXCELLENCE

Talent is long patience.

Gustave Flaubert

We all know about the lightbulb, but did you know that Thomas Edison also invented the stock ticker, the electric vote recorder, the automatic telegraph, the electric safety miner's lamp, fluorescent lights, the motion picture camera, and the phonograph?

Here is what he had to say while struggling with the lightbulb: "I have not failed seven hundred times. I have not failed once. I have succeeded in proving that those seven hundred ways will not work. When I have eliminated the ways that will not work, I will find the way that will work."

I've been thinking about patience for years now, but it is only in the past few months that I have come to see the connection between patience and the cultivation of excellence. Here's how Eric Hoffer puts it: "At the core of every true talent there is an awareness of the difficulties inherent in any achievement, and the confidence that by persistence and patience something worthwhile will be realized. Thus talent is a species of vigor." George Louis Leclerc de Buffon was referring to the same thing when he wrote, "Genius is nothing but a greater aptitude for patience."

These thinkers are reminding us that genius must be cultivated. "Raw" talent gets us only so far—we must work at a gift over and over again: painting, writing, computer know-how, golfing, love, parenting. Anything that we could potentially become good at requires that we dedicate ourselves to long effort. This is only possible when we are patient with our progress, no matter how slow or fast it may be.

A recent study confirms this. A researcher at the University of Florida discovered that, on average, it takes ten years of practice to acquire the mastery of an expert. That's a lot of patience!

A couple of years ago, the Gallup Organization released groundbreaking research in excellence. What they discovered, in a study of 2 million individuals, is that people who excel know what they are good at and practice even more in it. They don't worry about their weaknesses, but instead work on their particular combination of strengths until they have maximized them. (By the way, according to their research, there are 33 million possible combinations of these strengths, which means *your* particular configuration is one in 33 million. Thus, with the power of persistence, you can be your own one-of-a-kind genius.)

Like a fine wine that gets better with time, we fulfill our potential with patience. Through it, we are able to offer our unique brand of excellence to the world. And that is no small thing, for the world desperately needs the best of what each and every one of us has to give.

PATIENCE BRINGS US INTO HARMONY
WITH THE CYCLES OF NATURE

The patience for waiting is possibly the greatest
wisdom of all: the wisdom to plant the seed
and let the tree bear its fruit.

John MacEnulty

I was working with a woman, let's call her Meredith, who had spent her life chasing the American dream: she had gone to an Ivy League school, landed a six-figure job, and climbed the ladder to upper management. Then, in her mid-forties, she looked back at her accomplishments and they felt pretty hollow. Nothing in her life except her role as a mother and wife seemed meaningful. She left her job and came to me to figure out what to do next.

One of the first things I helped her see was that, like all living things, people go through seasons—the spring of new possibilities, where everything seems exciting and fresh; the summer of fruition, when you are in the full blossom of energy and creativity; the fall of disenchantment when you begin to lose interest; and the winter of discontent when you feel empty, afraid you will never be engaged with life again. She was in winter.

This is a natural process that we all go through, but because we are so used to thinking of ourselves as outside of nature, we are not aware of this cycle. So we try to stay in summer and medicate, distract, or otherwise prevent ourselves from going into fall or winter.

But this cycle is the growth process—for human beings as well as cucumbers and crocuses—and unless we allow ourselves to be in each season as it comes, we will never grow. For it is only in shedding our old ways of being, our old priorities and concerns, that we make room for the new.

As any gardener will tell you, the cycles of nature require patience. You can't just plant a seed and expect it to flower the next day. You can't tug on the leaves or unfurl the bud to hurry the process. Even a fast-growing vegetable like a radish requires time.

So do we. When we practice patience, we come more into alignment with the natural rhythms of life. We remember that "to everything there is a season," and we stop pushing for life to be different than it is. Winter takes as long as it takes, but it always ends—and so does summer. That's the law of nature.

That's what I told Meredith when she asked me despairingly one day when her internal winter would be over. I said I didn't know, but I did know it would end and that, just like a gardener, there were some things she could do to prepare for spring. Things like looking at what really mattered to her, what gifts she had, and what legacy she wanted to leave. Winter is the ideal time to prepare for what is to come, even if you don't know quite what that is yet.

She and I talked together for about a year. She worked hard on herself and cultivated her patience. Finally she got excited about a new business possibility and went off to pursue it. One day soon after, I got a card in the mail. It was one of those greeting cards that have flower seeds imbedded in the paper. Along with it came a note: "Thank you for holding the faith that spring would come again for me when I couldn't. These seeds represent those you helped me find when there seemed to be none."

We are living systems, a part of nature and as much subject to its cycles as the mightiest oak or the tiniest tree frog. Patience helps us feel that connection.

PATIENCE HELPS US MAKE
BETTER DECISIONS

A handful of patience is worth more
than a bushel of brains.

Dutch proverb

It was the middle of the night. My daughter, Ana, age two, had a high fever. We had given her Tylenol, and put her down to sleep between us. She woke up about a half hour later, crying. I panicked, yelling to my husband beside me to run and get the thermometer in the bathroom (about five steps away). Don sauntered to the bathroom and back; calmly he checked her temperature. It hadn't risen. Mine had though—I was furious!

As soon as Ana fell back to sleep, I lit into Don. "I can't believe you moved so slowly. This was an emergency! You couldn't hurry even if your life, or your daughter's, depended on it!"

Quietly, he responded. "She was hysterical and you were alarmed. It seemed that the best thing for me to do was to stay as calm as possible. I would not have gotten the thermometer any faster by running and I might have added to the general upset. Doing it my way took less than a minute total."

I looked at him. He was calm, focused. As for me, my heart was racing, I was sweating, and I felt like bursting into tears. It was obvious even to me, in my agitated state, that between the two of us, the person best equipped to deal with an emergency in that moment was Don. I knew from my years as a teenage lifeguard, when I dealt with all kinds of bloody accidents, that in a crisis it's much better to be composed than flapping around in a panic. Otherwise your feelings are swamping the rational part of your brain that can make sound decisions.

If I had been able to keep my patience and not launch into crisis mode, I would have been much more useful to Ana in the moment, and better able to decide whether to rush her to a hospital or help her go back to sleep. Rather than waiting sixty seconds for the facts—her temperature had not risen—I told myself something terrible was happening and set off my inner panic button.

Patience helps us make better decisions because it keeps us out of scary stories that cloud our judgment. At the end of the wonderful movie *Amelie*, there's a hilarious scene where she's finally reaching out to the man she loves and has sent him a message to meet her at a certain time and place. He doesn't show. Amelie decides there are two possibilities why: (1) He didn't get her message. (2) He was run over by a car, in a train wreck, shot, kidnapped, and sent to Afghanistan, only to end up alone on a mountaintop. It's a great moment because we can all relate. Scaring ourselves with disastrous scenarios is so typically human—and so injurious to our capacity to make good choices.

With patience, we approach life like this: something is happening, it may have a bad outcome, but then again it might not. Good or bad, I can deal with it. Getting upset about it will only make it worse, particularly in advance. As Mark Twain once said, "The worst troubles I've had in my life are the ones that never happened."

I don't know about you, but I have spent a great deal of time fretting over things that never came to pass because I wasn't able to wait calmly to see how things turned out. So it's been a great relief to me to find that the more I develop my patience, the calmer I feel. And the calmer I feel, the better I am able to gather the data before spiraling into unnecessary worry and panic.

If practicing patience brings me no other reward than the ability to make better decisions, particularly in a crisis, it will have been well worth the effort.

PATIENCE CONNECTS US TO HOPE

Patience is the art of hoping.

Luc de Vauvenargues

Jailed for fighting against apartheid, Nelson Mandela spent twenty-seven years in South African prisons. In all those long years, in degrading conditions of abuse and starvation (upon his arrival on the infamous Robbins Island prison, guards urinated on him and said, "Here you will die"), he never turned bitter toward whites. He never gave up on his dream of a society in which blacks and whites could live in freedom and harmony. And he never stopped hoping that someday he would be released.

He believed, he wrote in a prison memoir, that "someday I would once again feel the grass under my feet and walk in the sunshine as a free man." To him, hope meant "keeping one's head pointed toward the sun, one's feet moving forward. There were many dark moments when my faith in humanity was sorely tested, but I would not and could not give myself up to despair."

It is a custom in his tribe that grandfathers name their grandchildren, and when his oldest daughter, whom he had not seen for almost two decades, gave birth to a girl, Nelson Mandela named her Azwie—Hope. "The name had special meaning for me," he wrote in his autobiography *Long Walk to Freedom*, "for during all my years in prison hope never left me—and now it never would. I was convinced that this child would be part of a new generation of South Africans for whom apartheid would be a distant memory."

After ten thousand days, at the age of seventy-one, Nelson Mandela was finally freed and went on to guide South Africa to true democracy, without the wholesale slaughter of whites by blacks that the minority white population feared. "I never lost hope that this great transformation would occur," said Mandela. "I always knew that deep down in every human heart, there is mercy and generosity . . . Man's goodness is a flame that can be hidden but never extinguished."

The life of Nelson Mandela is one of the greatest examples of the power of patience. With calm persistence, he helped bring about a miracle not only for himself, but also for the 43 million other blacks and whites who inhabit South Africa. In his presidential inaugural speech, he praised the "ordinary, humble people of this country. You have shown such a calm, patient determination to reclaim this country as your own." He could have been talking about himself.

Under extreme duress, Nelson Mandela was able to tap into something profound in the human spirit: our capacity to hope, which allows us to work patiently toward a goal that we may never see.

"If we hope for what we don't see, we wait for it with patience," says Romans 8:25. With hope, we have the patience to work for what we want in our lives—to study for the test, write the book, make the quilt, plant the garden—because we trust in the possibility of a good outcome. Without hope, we would try nothing, do nothing, because we wouldn't have the emotional and spiritual wherewithal to apply the necessary elbow grease and wait upon the results.

Scientific research has confirmed the connection between hope and patience. Students who score high on a hope index do better as college freshmen than their low-hope peers, though they have the same range of intellectual abilities. The reason has to do with persistence—hope gave them the willingness to keep on trying. In another study, high- and low-hope students were given a hypothetical situation: you were aiming for a B in this course. On your first test, which represents 30 percent of your final grade, you got a D.

Now what do you do? The high-hope students came up with all kinds of ideas to raise their grade; low-hope students gave up.

Author Iyanla Vanzant encourages us to remember "that a delay is not a denial." What is your heart's desire? Is it worth hoping for? With patience, we nurture hope in the darkness of our waiting, so that one day our heart's desire may burst forth, fully realized.

PATIENCE HELPS US LIVE LONGER

AND MORE STRESS-FREE

Your biography becomes your biology.

Caroline Myss

A friend was visiting. An advisor to the CEO of a large corporation, he had a very stressful job—which he had just decided to quit. "It's killing me," he confided. "My blood pressure is through the roof and I am thoroughly burned out. I ignored my body as long as I could, but when my doctor warned me that I was at risk of having a heart attack, I paid attention. All I do is fight with [the CEO], pushing for what I think is right. And then he ignores my recommendations anyway. I've lost my tolerance for it."

I could not find any research into the physiological effects of patience. But there are many studies on the effects of impatience, particularly stress and anger. Research demonstrates that angry folks are one and a half times more likely to get cancer than others and have a four to five times higher risk of heart disease. The biological effects of anger and stress include increased heart rate, surging blood pressure, and more stomach acid, whether you suppress or express your feelings.

If you do vent, your brain gets even more worked up, sending the stress hormones adrenaline and cortisol surging through your bloodstream to prepare you to fight. This, scientists have found, has the effect of weakening your immune system, particularly your T-cells, which are the body's main infection fighters. Muscles contract, blood vessels constrict, and your heart has to work harder to circulate your blood. That's why you have the sensation of a pounding heart.

Conversely, when you are calm, your fight-or-flight system turns off. Your muscles relax, your blood vessels dilate, your blood pressure drops, your heart rate slows. Your immune system functions well again, producing the requisite number of T-cells, which ward off disease and help you live a longer, healthier life.

Patience allows us to keep our cool under stress, whether it is the external stress of our busy lives or the internal stress of anger. It takes the foot off the accelerator of your nervous system and allows it to rest. As Robert Sapolsky points out in *Why Zebras Don't Get Ulcers*, the fight-or-flight response is an important one for our survival—it helps us run away from danger, for instance. But it is designed for short bursts, not to be chronically on.

Given our current lifestyles, we could be experiencing fight-or-flight almost all the time—in traffic, under a tight work deadline, in spats with loved ones—which puts a great deal of strain on our bodies. That's why cultivating patience is one of the best things we can do for our health. The more we can easily roll with the punches of life and tolerate the quirks of other human beings, the less stress we will experience. And if that means one less day a week at the gym, won't that be a gift!

PATIENCE HELPS US WASTE LESS TIME, ENERGY, AND MONEY

> With time and patience the mulberry leaf
> becomes a silk gown.
>
> *Chinese proverb*

Years ago, the man I was living with and I built a house on a steep upslope lot. Actually, he built the house and I worked to support the family. The only part he didn't do himself was the foundation. The contractor slated to do the foundation work was overcommitted. In a rush to finish before the rains came, he didn't make it square or put it in the place on the lot where it should have been. And in a rush to get started before the rains came, we didn't check it.

If you were to visit that house now, you'd see a wall rising forty feet in the air, with a big step in it about one third of the way up to accommodate the fact that the foundation was out of plumb. That error cost us—in aesthetics and in trouble with the neighbors because the house wasn't located on the agreed upon spot. We ended up in years-long wrangles that took time, money, and energy.

That was a very big error brought on by lack of patience. But I experience all sorts of little ones all the time. I do something in a hurry, cut corners, make a mistake, and then have to start all over again.

It happened again last night. In my usual rush, I was putting together a complicated mango dressing for dinner. The last ingredient was salt. Not paying close enough attention, I put in way too much. I ended up having to throw the dressing away and start over again. Then I was not only annoyed that I had lost time, but aggravated at myself for rushing in the first place.

That was a silly error that cost me about ten minutes and one dollar. But how much time and money do we lose collectively through impatience? NASA comes to mind. Rushing on a project, they did some of their calculations in centimeters and some in inches, so a multimillion-dollar satellite completely missed its target. Oops!

These days we value speed so much that we now take such colossal errors for granted. Think of the media, which jumps to conclusions on stories before the facts are even in. "Dewey Wins!" is the famous blooper, but remember the flip-flopping on Election Night 2000? The TV networks just couldn't tolerate not declaring a presidential winner. Software manufacturers now, as a matter of course, put out programs they know are bug-filled and respond to customer complaints, rather than taking the time to work the kinks out first. Why? Because impatient investors will cause their stock price to plummet if they announce that they are not going to make their deadline.

Impatience can hurt us physically too. "Whenever I injure myself," a woman wrote to me, "I can invariably look back and see that it happened while I was rushing. I sprained an ankle running for the bus. I pulled out my back racing through a workout, trying to get to the office ten minutes sooner. Both injuries ended up taking much more time than the few minutes I was rushing to save."

It takes awareness to buck the fastness trend. But there are benefits. Remember the old adage "Haste makes waste"? It's as true now as the day it was coined. That's because, as my email correspondent pointed out, hurrying ends up taking more time because we make mistakes that we wouldn't have made if we'd just calmed down a little bit.

Given the hurry-up way we all live, perhaps we'd do well to change that old adage into one I heard recently from a wise woman, "Make haste—slowly."

PATIENCE GETS US MORE OF

WHAT WE WANT

You can catch more flies with
honey than vinegar.

Anonymous

I was standing in line in Toronto, Canada, waiting to clear U.S. customs and fly home. My flight was due to take off in an hour and the line was moving slowly. Very slowly. I had been away for five days and my daughter, back home with a cold, was missing me terribly. The old me would have fumed and fussed, making myself and all those around me miserable.

This time, however, I decided to try an experiment. What would happen if I acted as though it would somehow work out? So I waited, inching along. After about thirty minutes, I struck up a conversation with the man in front of me. "At least we're almost there," I remarked, eyeing the door ahead of us. "Oh no," he said, "this is just the line to get into the line."

About that time, a customs official came by to explain that their computers had been going on and off all day and that was why it was taking so long. I told myself to remain calm, holding the possibility of a good outcome. At fifteen minutes before takeoff, the customs officials called out, "All those going to Denver, over here." Off I went to wait in a shorter line.

Finally it was my turn. I walked up to the young woman at the computer. She looked tired. Very tired. I felt a surge of sympathy and I found myself saying, "Rough day, huh?" "Yup," she replied, stamping my passport and waving me onward.

It was only then that I noticed that her computer screen was black. Her computer was down and she should have made me wait until it came back on to verify my passport. Because I had been kind to her, she let me through—just in time for me to make my plane.

That incident won't leave me alone. It made me see that when we practice patience, we increase the chances we will get what we want. That's because when we're patient, we treat other people decently, which in turn increases the possibility that they will respond in kind.

I was reminded of this recently when a friend told me of an experience she had with a repairman. Unhappy with the work he'd done, she wanted a refund. She had called up and yelled at the company, eventually hanging up on the person on the other end. "I then called my husband," she reported, "who has more patience than I. He called, spoke calmly to the manager, and, surprise, got our money back."

Since my customs incident, I've heard all kinds of stories about how patience will get you what you want: the man who got his computer back after leaving it in a plane seat pocket by being gracious to the ten airline folks he had to speak to in order to get to the right person; the owner of a crowded restaurant who jumped customers to the head of the line because they were nice about waiting; the couple who got their checking account fee waived because they were kind in dealing with a banking snafu.

I used to believe that the adage "The squeaky wheel gets the grease" was the one to follow, and boy was I squeaky. Now I realize that often all the squeaky wheel gets is a wide berth or a swift kick. These days, I'm using my patience to spread around more honey than vinegar and the results are much sweeter.

PATIENCE GUARDS THE
DOOR TO ANGER

Patience is the ability to idle your motor when
you feel like stripping your gears.

Michael LeFan

It was one of those grocery store moments that you've likely witnessed. A mother, exhausted by a hard day of work and needing to pick up something for dinner, is racing through the aisles, three-year-old in tow. The child, hungry and tired, is pitching a fit. He wants a certain cereal that his mother has already vetoed for being too sugary. "I *want* too much sugar, I *want* too much sugar," he yells, throwing himself down on the ground. Mom snaps, yanking him up by the arm and dragging him out of the store. Mom, son, and the shoppers observing the scene end up upset.

It was only when I began to study patience closely that I came to see how anger and patience are related. In fact, anger is the direct consequence of losing our patience. For it is precisely because we don't have tolerance for something or someone that we get mad: "Why must you crack your knuckles when you know it drives me crazy?" "Why do you say 'lovely' in that simpering voice to everything that happens?" "Why is the health insurance system in this country so screwed up that I can't get a policy for under $800 a month?" We're angry because we don't want to put up with it.

This was a big "aha" for me. I knew that I was often impatient and that I lost my temper sometimes. But I had no idea that the two were related. They seemed like separate weather systems, operating independently of one another. But actually impatience is a continuum, beginning with irritation, leading to anger, and ending in rage.

What that means is that the converse is also true. The more patience we have, the less irritation, anger, and rage we'll experience. If the poor mother in the grocery store had been able to summon a bit more patience, she could have avoided striking out. Perhaps she could have laughed at the absurdity of her son's request for "too much sugar," offered a distraction, or just stood there calmly until his tantrum ran its course. Any of those options would have been better—for him and for her.

This is not to say that all anger is bad. We should never put up with exploitation or abuse, and our impatience in that regard is a healthy warning signal that our limits have been violated and we need to seek a safe haven. And there's also virtuous anger when it comes to injustice of all sorts, including, for instance, the inequities of the U.S. health care system, that fuels social change.

What I'm talking about here is the normal irritation and anger we feel toward people, places, or events in our daily lives that come from a lack of reasonable tolerance. You know what I mean—the patience we need to deal with our parents when they seem not to care at all about what matters to us; the serenity to deal with our children when they're pushing for an ice cream cone or a tattoo after we've said no four times; the persistence to keep on trying with a boss who doesn't seem to value our work. Or even the patience to enlist someone to help with our health care problem rather than yelling at the poor person at the end of the telephone line. When we employ patience, we are much better judges of when it is time to rise up in righteous anger and when we should grin and bear something.

There's an Irish proverb that goes something like this: "When you are angry, you're carrying the burden while the other person is out dancing." The more we cultivate patience, the less anger we carry and the more dancing we'll feel like doing.

PATIENCE GIVES US GREATER
TOLERANCE AND EMPATHY

If the person you are talking to doesn't appear to be listening,
be patient. It may simply be that he has
a small piece of fluff in his ear.

Pooh's Little Instruction Book

I was leading a training session in diversity of thinking for a Fortune 100 company. I was explaining that, although we all have the same equipment—a brain—we don't all use it in the same way. Rather, each of us takes in and expresses the world in a unique way. Understanding those differences goes a long way toward explaining a lot of what frustrates us about colleagues, bosses, spouses, and kids.

A hand flew up. "You mean," drawled one kindly gentleman from Louisiana, "my son isn't trying to defy me when he won't look me in the eye when I talk to him? And my boss isn't a jerk for not responding to my memos? That if I gave him my ideas verbally I'd have a much greater chance of success?"

"Yes," I replied, "that's exactly what I mean."

In the course of going about our business—at work, at home, at the grocery store, at community functions and private dinner parties—we bump up against people every day. And lo and behold—they're different from us. Not just in the ways that their brains take in information. They also have different priorities, motivations, histories, and cultures. We all know this in theory and in the name of tolerance, we say that it's good. But in fact, many of us don't really believe it. Consequently, we spend a great deal of energy trying to get the rest of the world to behave as we believe they should.

Remember the song from *My Fair Lady*, "Why Can't a Woman Be More Like a Man?" It could be our personal anthem with a slight variation, "Why Can't Everyone Be More Like Me?" Alas, they are not and that's where patience comes in. It helps you to graciously put up with the differences between you and everyone else you come across.

This tolerance can be a challenge. It requires stepping back from our assumptions of how the other person should be and inquiring how they actually are. But we have a great ally in this process.

It turns out that patience, that calm inner steadiness in the face of what might otherwise annoy us, is the gateway to empathy, the capacity to be aware of the feelings of others. That's because, says

Daniel Goleman in *Emotional Intelligence*, "Empathy requires enough calm and receptivity so that the subtle signals of feeling from another person can be received and mimicked by one's own emotional brain." In other words, the more patience we have, the greater our ability to feel for others.

With empathy, we get to see the other person for who he or she is in all his or her unique magnificence instead of trying to turn a person into someone else. Rather than being annoyed, for instance, that your teammate Fred moves so slowly, you can ask yourself what good might come from this trait. When you do, you see that he takes great care with everything he does and that's what his slowness is about.

This capacity, through patience, for empathy, has tremendous implications not only for us as individuals, but also as a global community trying to live together in peace. It is, argues researcher Martin Hoffman, the very basis of morality. For it is precisely because we can feel the pain and understand the position of others that we adhere to moral principles at all.

In this way, patience allows us to live more harmoniously—with family members who may be different, with neighbors who may have dissimilar priorities, with diverse teammates with whom we must work. Patience gives us a greater sense of wonder at the variety of human nature and a much greater capacity to open our hearts to it all.

PATIENCE HELPS US HAVE HAPPIER LOVE RELATIONSHIPS

Love is patient and kind.

*St. Paul, First Letter
to the Corinthians*

I have a friend who's a genius at falling in love. A tragic romantic, she calls herself. She has no trouble attracting a man, swooning in deep infatuation, and then rejecting him for some fatal flaw: too young, too short, not making enough money. She once told me that she couldn't marry this guy she was seeing because he left wet towels on the bathroom floor!

I used to consider some of her reasons to be silly, but eventually I came to see them as shorthand for this truth: she didn't love the person enough to put up with their flaws. None of them, for whatever reason, triggered her capacity for patience.

Fundamentally, you can't love without patience. Oh, as my friend experienced over and over, you can have the blush of first romance, that feel-good time when your brain is flooding your body with endorphins and all things between you feel possible. But when that glow fades and you, with all your idiosyncrasies, are face-to-face with this other human being with all of his or her idiosyncrasies and you are trying to negotiate a life together—that's when the rubber meets the road, patience-wise.

Over the long haul of a relationship, we each spend a great deal of time bearing with one another's faults: the fact that he belches in public; that she has periodic freak-outs over money; that his clothes never match and he's been wearing those shoes for over ten years; that she gets on the phone with friends as soon as she walks in the door rather than greeting you with a kiss.

People can and do change, but they rarely change as much as we desire. The secret to happiness in love may be to appreciate as delightful those little foibles that otherwise can be so annoying. Short of that heroic feat, which many of us never quite manage, it helps to haul out wheelbarrows full of patience for the times when he tells that old joke you've heard two thousand times before or when she comes home from yet another shopping spree.

What's fascinating about patience in love is that when we accept one another as we are, we actually increase the possibility of change. That's because our partner's patience produces a safe haven where we are accepted, warts and all, and in the warmth of that acceptance we may actually feel safe enough to risk growing. Thus, our partner may even end up changing in the ways we desire, precisely because we have given them the space to do so.

Patience also increases the chances that our relationships will last over the long haul. In a study of adults who had been high school underachievers (characterized by low persistence), it was found that they were 50 percent more likely to divorce in the thirteen years after high school than their classmates. In other words, people who don't use patience in one arena of their lives tend to give up on love sooner than those who learned stick-to-it-ness somewhere.

Patience is the mortar that holds love together, smoothing the surface between us so that love—and growth—can flourish.

PATIENCE MAKES US

BETTER PARENTS

God sends children for another purpose than merely to keep up the
race—to enlarge our hearts; and to make us unselfish and full of kindly
sympathies and affection; to give our shoulds higher aims; to call out
all our faculties to extended enterprise and exertion.

Mary Howitt

A busy journalist dad was trying to get his three-year-old daughter
off to preschool on time. "I was getting impatient because she was
laughing instead of putting on her socks. Finally I lost my temper
and shouted, 'Come on. I'm serious. No more laughing.' 'C'mon,'
she scolded in reply, wagging her finger at me as I had done and
mimicking my frowning face exactly. 'I'm very serious. No more
laughing.'

"At that moment I realized just how far I'd gone, valuing speed
over joy, and her serious act struck me as so hilarious that I started
laughing myself. 'Now look who's laughing,' she deadpanned."

Is there anything as cute as kids? They say such endearing things, cover you with kisses and hugs, want so badly to please you. Just being around them is a joy.

Is there anything as exasperating as kids? They spill grape juice on your brand new white carpet, ask the same questions over and over, and turn the ordinary tasks of living such as brushing teeth into ongoing power struggles. Just being around them is a pain.

As every parent knows, raising children requires a smorgasbord of capacities. We must be teachers, disciplinarians, coaches, friends—and know when each of these needs to make an appearance. And we must often make split-second decisions as to how to respond while juggling a thousand other things.

If that weren't pressure enough, because we live in psychologically aware times, we know more about the damage we have the potential to inflict. One hundred years of research into emotional development reveal that we parents determine, at least to some degree, whether our children end up being high-functioning human beings with the capacity to succeed in love and work—or not.

One of our greatest allies in this complex process of parenting is patience. Patience allows us to continue rocking a child who's been crying for an hour, to read *Horton Hears a Who* for the four hundredth time, to respond calmly as our teen arrives home from a sleepover with purple hair.

I haven't known one day as a parent that my patience hasn't been tried—and I have a very easygoing child. Testing just goes with the territory. By the very nature of childhood, parents and children spend their lives together engaged in a struggle: children to constantly test how far they can go; parents to create a safe circle and expand it wisely as our children grow in maturity.

That's why patience is the pause that refreshes. It allows us to stop in this battle between independence and safety and assess what the best response might be. It allows us to think before we act, which is crucial in this relationship where we have such power.

Our kids are asking us for greater patience. In a 1999 study on work-life balance by Ellen Galinsky, it was found that the one thing most children wished they could change about their parents was that they be less stressed out when they get home from work.

No matter how hard we might try, we'll not be perfect parents. And that's OK—all we really need to do is to be good enough. Patience helps us be good enough—good enough so that our kind, loving, and wise responses outweigh our sharp, ill-considered ones.

PATIENCE TEACHES THE POWER
OF RECEPTIVITY

Patience [is one of those] "feminine" qualities which
have their origin in our oppression but
should be preserved after our liberation.

Simone de Beauvoir

Mary Beth lost her job on her forty-third birthday. The prior two
years had been very difficult. Her marriage had ended. A magazine
she had launched failed the year before. She was trying frantically
to put her life back into some semblance of financial order, so the
news of her unemployment struck hard.

"I had no job, three kids in Catholic schools, and a mortgage. I
spent a month in a frenzy sending out resumes, calling colleagues,
scouring ads. Nothing. The harder I searched, the more frustrating
it became.

"Then, one September morning, I just stopped. I woke up, took my coffee out to my garden, and prayed: God, I've tried everything. It's in your hands now, whatever is meant for me. I decided that all I could do was to be receptive to whatever happened. I wrote stories and sent them off, unsolicited, to editors. Nothing happened. For months, after I got the kids off to school, I headed out to my garden to spend an hour in prayer, waiting. I waited long after my pumpkins were harvested, until a pink geranium put forth its last single bloom in December, until the whole garden became barren. I waited and prayed. I kept writing.

"Finally, in January, a dream job opened for me. By spring, all the stories I had written in the fall began appearing and the checks were in my mailbox again."

When I first began to study patience, I was struck by how wimpy it seemed. Unlike kindness, gratitude, or generosity, which are about things you do, this quality is a lot about what you *don't* do. It's about holding back when you want to let loose, putting up with something you'd rather not, and waiting for something to happen rather than forcing it along.

As I thought more deeply, though, I began to see how my attitude was very much a reflection of the culture at large, one that values action above all else. As Americans we are all about doing: conquering the mountain; dominating the market; making money as quickly as possible; climbing to the top of the career ladder.

These all represent action-oriented, dynamic activities, the energy of the masculine, as it were.

What we tend not to value in our culture are the more receptive, "feminine" activities: waiting on heaven; opening to intuition; listening for the right moment; allowing truth to penetrate and move us. Patience, as Simone de Beauvoir points out, belongs in the receptive range of responses.

There is absolutely nothing wrong with dynamic energy—we need it to bring about anything at all in the world. But we've gotten into a state of imbalance as individuals and as a society because we only value dynamic energy. We have little or no appreciation for the receptive, which is the place where we stop to reflect, to judge whether action is appropriate or not, to wait for the right timing. We think we're not "doing" anything when we are receptive.

However, the receptive energy of patience is real work! It takes effort to not simply run off and do something for the sake of doing it, to live in the unknown for as long as it takes without becoming angry, bitter, or depressed. It may look like nothing on the surface. But underneath, within ourselves, we're lifting some heavy timber. Taoists call this *wu wei*, actionless activity, also translated as "sitting quietly doing nothing." In ancient China, *wu wei* was valued as one of the highest human achievements possible.

Mary Beth's story is powerful because, as it demonstrates, sometimes no amount of dynamic energy will get us what we want.

At those times, all we can do is stop and wait patiently for the future to unfold. This capacity to wait expectantly, opening ourselves up to help from God or the universe, is what receptivity is all about.

Not everything can be accomplished through willpower—sometimes what we need is a bit of wait power.

PATIENCE IS THE HEART
OF CIVILITY

Patience furthers.

Lama Surya Das

A few years ago, a friend became mayor of her city of twenty-five thousand. She invited me to her swearing-in party, which was at the end of the regular city council meeting. I went early, sat through the meeting, and was soon overcome with admiration. What patience these city officials have to go through the same problems over and over again, trying to meet urgent needs with little money, pushed on all sides by special interest groups advocating for their position! I could tell in this one meeting that the issues on the table had been hashed and rehashed many times, but everyone treated one another with respect, and every citizen who wanted to be heard was, whether what they had to say was on the topic or not.

By the end of the evening, I inwardly bowed in awe toward all public officials for their patience with the process of government, as well as all those tireless citizen activists who unflaggingly advocate for what they believe is right. Then I began to think about the so many others who patiently work to keep our society together—all those laboring for pennies in nonprofits, police and firefighters, peace workers around the world, the list goes on and on.

I contrast those folks with people in a story that the newspapers recently have been filled with. After a van careened into a sidewalk injuring three pedestrians, seven men pulled the driver and passenger out of the van and beat them to death. This happened in a middle-income neighborhood in Chicago; the men accused of murder range in age from sixteen to forty-seven.

When I contemplate this horrific story from the lens of patience, what I'm struck by is not that it happened, but that it doesn't happen more often. These men couldn't wait for justice to take its course (the driver, a sixty-two-year-old man, was drunk), and instead took matters into their own hands, meting out their own form of "punishment." It's newsworthy because it is unusual, since most of us, even those who have been harmed, have learned to wait on society's processes and procedures.

Indeed it is because most of us are able to use patience that society functions at all. Because we are willing to be patient, we wait for the lights to turn green before we go rather than running the red; we wait calmly when going to a large event like a ball game or a concert, rather than trampling people to get in; we wait on our government to solve problems to the best of its ability rather than plotting an overthrow.

To the extent that we employ patience, society holds together, with the billions of us alive on the planet today going about the business of living in a more or less orderly and lawful way. It is when we become impatient—whether for a quick buck as in the corporate greed fest of the late nineties or in our cars on a crowded freeway—that lawlessness breaks out.

Patience is no small, feel-good personal quality. It is at the heart of diplomacy and civility, lawfulness and civil order. Without it, people can't work together and society can't function at all. With it, we create the possibility of peace between people and between nations.

PATIENCE GROWS OUR SOULS

We could never learn to be brave and patient,
if there were only joy in the world.

Helen Keller

In her book *Kitchen Table Wisdom*, Rachel Naomi Remen tells the story of a surly teenage boy who was struggling with a diagnosis of childhood diabetes. He was acting out—not eating properly, not taking his medication. Then, one day, he came to her office, smiling. He'd had a dream. He told her, "In my dream, I saw a statue of a young Buddha. Just looking at it made me feel peaceful. Then, out of nowhere, a dagger came from behind me and went right into the heart of the Buddha. I was shocked, devastated. Then, as I watched, upset and angry, the Buddha began to grow. He grew and grew until he was the size of a giant. The knife was still there, but compared to the Buddha, it now was only the size of a toothpick."

I have two friends who say that breast cancer was the best thing that happened to them; one who says her husband leaving her was a blessing in disguise; another who claims losing her job was the greatest gift. Are these folks all masochists? No, these are ordinary folks, like that young dreamer, who realize that the trials they faced, as difficult, painful, and grueling as they were, have been the vehicles by which they have grown into more awake and aware human beings. "When I planted my pain in the field of patience," wrote Kahlil Gibran, "it bore fruit of happiness."

Cancer survivor and bicycling champion Lance Armstrong puts it this way: "The truth is that cancer was the best thing that ever happened to me. . . . When I was sick, I saw more beauty and triumph and truth in a single day than I ever did in a bike race. . . . The one thing the illness has convinced me of beyond all doubt, more than any experience I've had as an athlete, is that we are much better than we know. We have unrealized capacities that sometimes only emerge in crisis."

None of us wants to have to suffer through physical, emotional, or spiritual hardships. But when such trials do come—and they most likely will, for each life has its measure of sorrow—we have two choices: to rail endlessly against what is happening or to experience our feelings of sorrow, fear, and anger, then engage our patience and allow the challenge to grow our souls.

Norman Vincent Peale refers to this when he writes: "When pain strikes, we often ask the wrong questions, such as Why me? The right questions are, What can I learn from this? What can I do about it? What can I accomplish in spite of it?"

When we meet up with frustration and pain, we are being called to move to a higher level in ourselves, to discover untapped inner resources. At a workshop I cofacilitate, my colleague Dawna Markova, author of *I Will Not Die an Unlived Life*, leads people through a personal reflection on the wisdom they've gleaned through some difficulty they've faced. They are asked to bring to mind one resource that allowed them to get through those times. We've done this with hundreds of folks and everyone can identify at least one inner resource they've cultivated as a result of a hardship.

Just as there is no rainbow without the rain, you have developed beautiful soul characteristics as a consequence of circumstances that tried your patience. Take a moment right now to reflect on what they are. (For me, it is my capacity to understand other people's perspectives and my belief in fundamental human goodness.) These resources will be with you for the rest of your life. And when a new challenge comes to test your patience, you can ask yourself how you are being called on to grow and therefore find the hardship a bit easier to bear.

3.

THE ATTITUDES OF PATIENCE

The greatest discovery of my generation is that a
human being can alter his life by altering his mind.

William James

We all have deeply ingrained attitudes about life, some of them
held below the level of our conscious awareness, that drive our responses to the people and circumstances we encounter. When
those attitudes are ones that foster patience, we experience tolerance, acceptance, and serenity. If they are attitudes that foster impatience, then we have little stomach for life's challenges.

Luckily, as Sylvia Boorstein puts it, "We are free to choose our
mind states." We are not blindly at the mercy of our thoughts, but

can make choices as to which attitudes to hold. This doesn't mean that we won't slip back into limiting beliefs, if we have them, for by now they are deep grooves in our brains. But each time we find that we have chosen a dead-end thought, we can begin again, reminding ourselves of the better options. After all, as Buddhist teacher Yvonne Rand reminds us, "An intention to cultivate patience is half the battle."

I'M STILL LEARNING

Awareness releases reality to change you.

Anthony de Mello

I was feeling terrible. I had just yelled at my husband about money, although I had promised myself going into the conversation that I would not lose my patience. I felt like a failure, a fraud.

The feeling was so familiar. Every time I told myself I should be more patient and then I wasn't, I felt awful. I would beat myself up for blowing it. And then I would vow not to do it again and all would be well—until the next time. Suddenly, seemingly out of the blue, the Impatient Ogre would rise up and lash out again. I would feel shame, take another vow, and the cycle would repeat itself.

I could have gone on this way until I gave up in despair, convinced I had no patience. Fortunately, however, I had help in the form of books and advice from friends. And that advice all had a common theme: what creates true change is becoming aware of what we are doing, without judging ourselves. Awareness allows us to learn. In other words, the way to cultivate more patience is to see ourselves as learners and each occasion of impatience as an opportunity to grow.

We're not always going to do it right. We're going to blow up at our mate, snap at our children, roll our eyes at a relative on the phone. We're going to honk our horn in frustration at the cars in front of us and make a federal case about a sock on the floor.

The question is not whether we lose our patience, but rather how we treat ourselves when we do. Do we berate ourselves for not being perfect? Or do we kindly acknowledge that we are still learning and wonder what we might learn from this?

Patience is enhanced by understanding *why* something is pushing our buttons, not by willpower. With willpower, we "try" to be good, but inevitably we fail, setting off shame, guilt—and no learning. In similar circumstances, we will do the same thing again.

When we see ourselves as learners, however, we acknowledge that something in the situation was hard for us, and we seek to understand what that is. With kindness toward ourselves, we open to the possibility of relating to a challenge differently next time.

The next time you find yourself losing it over something, try asking, I wonder what was hard for me about that? rather than thinking, I'm a bad person. Here are some thoughts about where to look. When we are impatient with someone, it might be because that person is allowing him- or herself something we don't permit ourselves to do. That was what was happening for a dad I know. His adult son was able to say no when he wanted to and Dad couldn't, so he lost his patience every time his son asserted himself.

Or perhaps the other person represents an aspect of ourselves that we've disowned. In psychological terms, this phenomenon is called projection. We get impatient with others who represent aspects of ourselves that we have pushed away or are angry we don't have.

When I look at my husband in this light, what I see is that I worry a lot about money and feel that Don should too. So I accused him of not acting responsibly when in fact he's very responsible. What made me see red was his peace of mind about money. What I really want is my own peace of mind regarding money and I was angry that he has it and I don't. This awareness doesn't mean that I never lose my cool around money issues, but I do it less now that I understand where my impatience is coming from.

There is a world of difference between feeling like a failure and feeling like you have something to learn. One leads to stuckness and despair, the other to possibility and growth. When your impatience buttons get pushed, try seeing it as an occasion to learn something about yourself. Ask, Why is this hard for me? You will be amazed at what such an attitude will produce.

PATIENCE IS A DECISION

If we love and cherish each other as much as we can
while we can, I am sure love and compassion
will triumph in the end.

Aung San Suu Kyi

Aung San Suu Kyi (her name means "a bright collection of strange victories") is an international symbol of nonviolent resistance to oppression. The leader of Burma's National League for Democracy, which won election in 1990 but has never been allowed to rule, she was the winner of the Nobel Peace Prize in 1991 for her "nonviolent struggle for democracy and human rights," a struggle the committee called "one of the most extraordinary examples of civil courage in Asia in recent decades."

To me, Aung San Suu Kyi is a model of patience. For much of the past fifteen years, she has been under house arrest at her home in Rangoon. She has not seen her children for over ten years; her husband died abroad in 1999 without her saying goodbye. The government refused to issue him a visa and she was afraid that if she left the country, she would not be allowed back in. When the Burmese military killed more peaceful protesters at a rally than the Chinese did in Tiananmen Square, when the military tortured, killed, or imprisoned thousands of her followers, she spoke out forcefully for democracy, but without hatred, bitterness, or vengefulness. Recently she said this about her captors: "We believe in talking to people, even those with whom we disagree. Actually it's more important to talk with people with whom we disagree, because it's precisely [with them that] we need to try to come to an understanding."

What allows her to keep her patience day in and day out? I wondered. She has a deep and abiding spiritual life, which has only grown in the times she has been under lock and key. But in *Letters from Burma*, she provides another clue: she understands that patience is a decision that we choose to make, not once, but over and over. As her house is blockaded or unblockaded, as soldiers mass outside her compound or issue new restrictions, she (and her followers, if they are allowed to enter) makes a conscious decision to continue patiently on. "We carry on with our work," she writes in one letter. In another: " 'Business as usual,' we chanted and carried on with our work." In yet another: "We go forward step by step, and we will keep on going forward step by step." Letter after letter, the pattern becomes clear: whatever obstacles are placed in her path, she acknowledges them and then decides to patiently move forward.

Patience is not something we either have or don't. It's a decision we make, a choice we take, again and again. And the more we recognize patience as a decision, the more we are free to make it. We decide to be patient when losing weight and rather than trying to lose "fifty pounds in a month" (as an ad I recently saw promised), we work steadily toward that goal and increase the likelihood of long-term success. We choose patience when trying to get pregnant and end up two years later with the miracle baby, as my friend did recently.

When we see patience as a decision, we understand that we will be faced, hopefully not in as difficult circumstances as Aung San Suu Kyi, with the choice over and over again. Each time, we are free to choose patience—with our maddening boss, our quarrelsome siblings, our exasperating neighbor.

The beauty of the decision for patience is that it doesn't matter how impatient we consider ourselves to be. We will always have another opportunity to choose! In whatever circumstance we find ourselves right now, we are free to choose peaceableness.

Each and every day, moment by moment, the decision is yours.

THIS TOO SHALL PASS

Long is not forever.

German proverb

Khyentse Norbu was a young Tibetan monk when Bernardo Bertolucci went to India to film *Little Buddha*, about Prince Siddhartha, who went on to become the Buddha. As an extra in the movie, Khyentse Norbu got bitten by the filmmaking bug and five years later, his independent film, *The Cup*, about a group of young monks' obsession with the World Soccer Championships, was released to great acclaim. Overnight, Khyentse Norbu became somewhat of a celebrity.

I read an interview with him shortly after this life-changing event. He spoke about the Buddhist concept of impermanence, the fact that everything changes, that nothing stays the same forever. Non-Buddhists think impermanence is a downer because it emphasizes loss, he said, but he sees it as positive as well. For without impermanence, he quipped, "I would fall into despair at the fact that I don't have a BMW. But impermanence means that my non-BMW state may change at any moment!"

I laughed when I read that and his remark has stuck with me. For when it comes to practicing patience, it helps a lot to remember that things always change. Even if they don't change as quickly as we want or in the ways we would like, what we can count on is that they will change.

When we are experiencing impatience, we tend to concretize current reality: it's like this and it's going to be this way forever. I'm going to be in this job forever; I'm going to be changing diapers forever; I'm going to be struggling financially forever; I'm going to be alone forever; I'm going to be in this bed sick forever. If we're in an uncomfortable situation, small or large, it's pretty easy for the world to narrow down to just that unpleasantness and for us to despair of it ever being over.

When we remember that things always change, we can hold on more comfortably. That's why I smiled when I came across the German proverb above: long *is* not forever, it only *feels* that way.

It isn't just Buddhists and Germans who have this teaching, of course. It was Jesus Christ who said, "This too shall pass." This profound truth is a great comfort when times are tough, for it gives us the strength and hope—and patience—to hang in there with what is.

THE SCREWS ARE JUST AS
IMPORTANT AS THE WINGS

We can do no great things;
only small things with great love.

Mother Teresa

Mother Teresa was visiting a factory in India when she happened to notice a man in the corner, happily humming and assembling screws. "What are you doing?" she asked. "Making airplanes," he replied. "Airplanes?" she inquired. "Yes," he said, "because without these tiny screws the plane cannot fly."

I love this story. It reminds me that when work feels like drudgery, it can help to remember our place in the overall scheme of things. This man understood the importance of his contribution, no matter how small, and therefore could patiently tackle his task.

So much of our lives at work can try our patience. Paying our dues, working our way through the system and up the ladder, handling bosses and coworkers. As a consultant to corporations massive and minute, I am always amazed at how resilient and positive people in organizational life are most of the time, despite the constant demands for increased productivity and doing more with less. Particularly in large companies, there seems to be almost perpetual restructuring—this year's new initiative that everyone must adopt, yet another reorganization of the way the entire business runs. While there may be grumbling and complaining, people generally roll up their sleeves and engage again. To do this, they must know they matter.

Fast Company once did a survey of the reasons why people stay with an organization. Money was reason number five. Number one was feeling valued. In order to be happy at work, we all need to feel we are contributing something of importance—to the bottom line, to promoting the goals of an organization, to a feeling of camaraderie. For each of us, how we wish to make a difference varies; what is similar is our longing to experience our value.

Ben Zander, conductor of the Boston Philharmonic writes of this in the book *The Art of Possibility*. There is, he says, in each of us "a universal desire to contribute to others, no matter how many barriers there are to its expression." When we trust our ability to contribute and when we validate the contributions of others, we increase patience at work—our own and that of those around us.

While we can be validated by others, ultimately, we must make our own meaning, as the Indian factory worker did. We must discover where our deep purpose and the needs of the world come together. From this place, we can work steadily toward our goal—a streamlined process, a startling innovation, higher collected revenue, greater morale. No longer needing to see immediate results, we can be like Michelangelo painting the Sistine Chapel on his back for four long years. Or the workers at the World Trade Center, patiently shifting through millions of tons of rubble to find a wedding ring, a set of keys—anything that loved ones could have as a reminder of those who died.

Where are you needed? What is the value you bring? What masterpiece are you being called to create, one screw at a time?

WAITING IS PART OF

BEING ALIVE

Let us, then, be up and doing,
With a heart for any fate;
Still achieving, still pursuing,
Learn to labour and to wait.

Henry Wadsworth Longfellow

In *There's a Spiritual Solution to Every Problem*, Wayne Dyer writes about flying to Greece to run in a race. His plane was delayed in New York for eight hours, during which time most of his fellow travelers roamed about, grumbling and complaining. Except for one little old Greek lady in her eighties who sat the whole time in one spot, "as peaceful as could be . . . showing no signs of dismay."

Once they boarded the plane, the woman was seated across from Wayne. "She smiled at me and then, believe it or not, for the next thirteen hours . . . she never moved once. She didn't eat, drink, get up, watch a movie, complain, stir—nothing but sit in the same position as in the departure area, with the same contented look on her face." When they finally landed in Greece, twenty-two hours after they began, she "was in an animated, high energy, joyful mood" as she greeted those waiting for her.

"To this day," he writes, twenty years later, "whenever I am involved in a similar delay situation I recall that little Greek lady all dressed in black and remind myself of how to enter and remain in a mind field of peace."

That lady in black knew something that many of us have forgotten—that much of life requires waiting and we have a choice to do it happily or miserably. It's a lesson I learned the hard way. I've had to travel a lot for work in the past two and a half years, and I hate it. Traveling more than anything means waiting in line: to board the airport shuttle, to go through airport security, to board the plane, to get off the plane, to get a rental car . . .

Recently my husband asked me why I instantly see red at the prospect of waiting in line. The answer eluded me until I read David Baily Harned's book called *Patience: How We Wait Upon the World*. And there it was in black and white: one of the assumptions of our impatient age is that "waiting is not at the core and center of human life but somehow *accidental*: we should not have to wait. Human progress should mean our emancipation from the necessity to wait, because science and technology have freed us from so many forms of dependence upon our natural environment." That's right, I thought. Society should have worked out all kinks so that there's no waiting anytime, anywhere!

I'm not alone in this belief, says Harned. Most of us alive today think waiting represents a flaw in some system, rather than a natural condition of life. But human beings have always had to wait—for good weather to plant crops, for plagues to end, for their loved ones to return from years at sea, never knowing if they were alive or not. The only difference now is what we wait on, not that we must.

In fact, warns this professor of religious studies, waiting on factors outside of our control is only going to increase as technology and complexity increase. Studies show the average person spends eleven days a year in line—and that doesn't count the number of hours in cars and on planes or wading through electronic voice mail to speak to a real live person. Technology doesn't reduce our waiting time—it just changes what we're waiting for.

Professor Harned helped me realize that, while certainly systems can be improved, waiting can never be completely eliminated from our lives. And the more that we accept this truth, like Wayne Dyer's Greek flier did, the happier we will be. Think on that the next time your blood begins to boil at an automated voice mail system, a trip to the post office, or when your computer freezes.

To live is, at least in part, to wait.

IT'S BETTER TO WORK AT IT THAN
TO BUY YOUR WAY OUT OF IT

I think and think for months and years,
ninety-nine times, the conclusion is false.
The hundredth time I am right.

Albert Einstein

The other day a friend gave Don and me a desktop computer he no longer needed. This computer could take a DSL line, making our connection much faster and freeing up a phone line. Great, we said. It's simple to install, we were told.

Unfortunately, like so much of life, it may have been simple, but it sure wasn't easy. Don fiddled and fiddled, spent time on the phone with our email provider, and then threw up his hands. "I can't figure it out," he moaned. "Let's just go out and buy a new computer."

Now I am a frugal New Englander and this went against all of my values, including patience. Why throw away a (perhaps) perfectly good computer because you are not willing to take the time to figure out how to make it work? "Call Damian," I suggested, referring to our computer genius stepson. "Please try again. I am not willing to give up yet." (Of course this was easy for me to say, I wasn't the one who had already spent three hours on it.)

While he went back to work, I ruminated. Don's response seemed typical. Everything in our culture supports such thinking. If something's not working, well, throw it away and get a new one. Don't worry about having patience, buy your way out of it. Buy a new water heater rather than fix the old one. Pay alimony rather than dig into the difficulties with your spouse.

Every day, advertisers bombard us with messages that life doesn't have to be unpleasant, difficult, or annoying if only you buy what they're selling. Use products instead of patience; new hard drives instead of hard work.

There are many problems with such an attitude, not the least of which is the crushing consumer debt we Americans are carrying. The average household credit card debt now stands at $8,367, according to *Money* magazine, and we spend 1.22 dollars for every dollar we make. But that's only the most obvious problem.

At a subtler level, our buying into this belief causes us to give up too soon, to miss out on the spiritual and emotional rewards that sticking with something offers. To work through a problem with our spouse rather than throw up our hands in despair; to try, like

Einstein in the above quote, one more time to solve a thorny dilemma; and yes, to stick with trying to make the computer work—these and countless other situations that require patience teach us about ourselves.

We learn that we are resourceful, competent, that we can count on ourselves when life challenges us. And when we do succeed, we experience a sense of accomplishment that could not have been gotten if we paid our way out of it.

That's what happened for Don. Two hours after proclaiming he was giving up, he figured it out. It didn't cost a penny, and the show he put on dancing around the bedroom in pride was priceless.

WHERE ARE YOU HURRYING TO?

The thing about the rat race is that even
if you win, you're still a rat.

Lily Tomlin

Denise is one of the most well-organized and speedy people I know. She doesn't waste a minute of time. As a consequence, she has accomplished a lot in her thirty-five years, including launching two start-up companies. But she was stopped in her tracks one Saturday morning.

"My husband and I were going to do errands together. In my efficient manner, I had divided the chores up into two lists, one for him and one for me. My thought was that we would each buzz through our list as fast as possible. As I handed him his list, his face fell. 'Oh,' he said. 'I thought the point was to do these things together.' A lightbulb flashed on in my head for about a minute, but I didn't really get it. I was too busy pushing ahead. Eventually he left me. Then I had lots of time to think. And I've come to see that the journey is as important as the destination."

Where are we hurrying to anyway? Did Denise want to spend time with her husband or get the chores done? So many of us are speeding around so quickly that we don't even bother to consider where we are trying to go or how what we are doing fits into what really matters to us.

"Are you the first to jump up and clean off the table?" asks Iyanla Vanzant. "We got stars for that in first grade. . . . The busyness started way back then. We were rewarded for doing more than our share. We were encouraged to stay busy." By adulthood, it's become a habit. We've become, in Iyanla's words "do-more-better-faster people." But are we enjoying our lives? No, she insists. "Trust me, do-more-better-faster people . . . do not enjoy working: we simply do not know how to stop."

What if there were a better answer than hurrying? It turns out there is. Sports psychologist Gary Mack counsels top athletes to make a 90 percent effort. When they do, they actually go faster. How come? Because voluntary muscles are organized into opposing pairs, like a brake and an accelerator going at the same time. With a 90 percent effort, athletes "expend a lot of muscular energy but they relax the antagonist muscles that hinder maximum performance," explains Mack. At 100 percent, the muscles are working against themselves.

What if you were to employ 90 percent effort in your life? "You don't always have to have something to do," says Iyanla. "When you do have something to do, do it at a pace that is comfortable to you . . . knowing that everything gets done in divine time and according to divine order."

If this perspective is challenging for you, remind yourself of The First Rule of Holes: "When you find yourself in a hole, the first rule is to stop digging." The next time you find yourself in a frazzle, stop. Stop digging, stop racing around, and ask yourself, Where am I hurrying to? Is it a destination that I truly care about? If so, how might I give 90 percent to get 100 percent results?

BOREDOM IS ALL IN

OUR HEADS

When people are bored it is primarily with
their own selves that they are bored.

Eric Hoffer

Ana has developed a new habit. Suddenly everything she doesn't
want to do comes with the label "boring." "That's boring," she'll
proclaim when I suggest we read a particular story or inform her
that we are going out to do errands. "It's too boring to wait," she
whines when I tell her I will attend to her needs in two minutes.
"Where did you learn that?" I ask, but she can't say. I think she
picked it up in the ethers.

Boredom as a lament is everywhere. Apparently there is no
greater crime in life these days than being bored. Waiting for food
to cook is boring—zap it in the microwave. Waiting for a movie

plot to unfold is boring—fast-forward the VCR. Reading a book from beginning to end is boring—hypertext on the Internet instead. We crave fast-paced Nintendo games, the blur of quick-cut music videos, TV programs with speeded up conversation (they've figured out technically how to do this by the way; dialogue on TV is now faster than the speaker's actual pace). We want, we need, constant stimulation—or else we're bored.

Such speed is fun, exhilarating. But it comes with a price tag. What happens to our ability to concentrate, to ponder deeply, to understand things within a context, to work hard today for that which will not bear fruit for many tomorrows?

The labeling of a huge part of human experience as boring is a relatively new phenomenon. The concept of boredom—a sense of emptiness and a lack of stimulation—didn't even exist until the nineteenth century. Before that, it was used only in the context of a person who spoke too long or rambled off the topic: "Oh, she's such a bore!" Now it is a state of being that is a fate worse than death.

Psychologists say that the problem we think is "out there"—in the book, movie, job, relationship—is actually in us. Boredom, they say, is created by an inability to delay gratification and a low tolerance for frustration, both of which have serious implications for our success in life and in love.

Any time we proclaim something boring, what we really are saying is that we don't have patience for it. Rather than looking at ourselves for the source of the problem—and therefore the solution—we look at whatever is provoking the feeling and label that the problem.

A lot of human experience can be considered boring. There are huge stretches in parenting, in relationships, in work, where "nothing" is happening, or at least nothing obvious. We can consider those moments boring and seek to alleviate that boredom with any distraction available. Or we can see such occasions as opportunities to tap into our patience and look more deeply.

Try it yourself. Go on a fast for a week in which you refuse to consider any experience boring. When your mind begins to use that label—in traffic, say, or on hold—challenge yourself to find something of interest in what is going on, either in yourself or the world around you. How does that change your experience?

With attention, nothing is boring, even the most routine tasks. If you tune in to how the warm soapy water feels on your hands as you wash the pots and pans, how does that change the experience for you? Or weeding the garden, how does it feel to bend and stretch in the sunlight? What *is* the name of that gray bird with the crested head that suddenly appeared? This level of experiencing life isn't one that we usually tune in to, but it is one that can bear many riches of wonder at the very fact of being alive in this amazing world.

REMEMBER RULE NUMBER SIX

Don't take it personally.

Don Miguel Ruiz

Two leaders are meeting, when an employee of Leader Number One comes bursting in, ranting and pounding his fist. Leader Number One says, "Kindly recall rule number six," whereupon the man instantly composes himself, apologizes, and leaves. This happens twice more. Finally Leader Number Two can't contain himself. "What is rule number six?" he asks. "Don't take yourself so damn seriously," replies Number One. "That's a fine rule," says Number Two. "What are the others?" "That's it," says Number One.

I loved that story when I came across a version of it in *The Art of Possibility*. It has so much to teach us about patience.

Have you ever noticed that the less patience a person has the more self-importance they seem to exhibit? I shouldn't have to put up with this, they seem to say, because I deserve better. I've got better places to be and better things to do. I am too important to wait. The universe revolves around me—or at least it should. "Don't you know who I am?" the very impatient dad of a friend used to thunder at waiters, clerks, and others whom he saw as obstacles in his path.

There's another great story in *The Art of Possibility* about this link between self-importance and impatience. The famous conductor Herbert von Karajan once jumped into a taxi and shouted to the driver to hurry up. "Where to?" asked the cab driver. "It doesn't matter," said von Karajan. "They need me everywhere."

For each of us, the task of growing up requires a balancing act between healthy self-esteem on the one hand and being too self-centered on the other, between understanding how wonderful we are and recognizing that the world doesn't revolve around us.

One of the reasons we experience impatience is because deep in the inner recesses of our hearts, we believe that life should always go our way, and that there is something terribly amiss if it doesn't. That belief comes from the infantile part of us for, as babies, it worked that way (or at least it should have). Our caregivers existed to meet our needs immediately and life really did revolve around us.

But relatively soon, they changed the rules on us. We had to fit into the larger program, whatever that meant in our particular family—dealing with siblings, set mealtimes, day care, etc.—and life was never the same. As we grow, we have to reconcile ourselves to the fact that as magnificent as we may be, we're not the center of the universe. And in some way we're still mourning that loss.

That's why when we experience impatience, it helps a lot to remind ourselves that it's *not* all about us and that what is happening is *not* personal. Life is just going impartially on its own way, and the more we align ourselves with the way it is going, the happier and more content we will be. When we remember rule number six, we can lighten up and roll a bit better with life's punches.

TUNING OUT IS AS IMPORTANT
AS TUNING IN

Better to get up late and be wide awake than to
get up early and be asleep all day.

Anonymous

I used to have an employee who was incredibly hard driving. Barbara prided herself on working longer hours than anyone and never taking any time off. I would have to force her to take vacations. My signal that she needed rest? She became impatient with customers and coworkers, less resilient to the irritations of her job.

How come it's so easy to see that kids become cranky because they are overtired and so hard to understand that the same thing may be true for us adults? I am convinced that much of our impatience comes from our never tuning out. Between emails, voice mails, beepers, and cell phones, we are never off duty. A survey by

Pitney Bowes found that 38 percent of workers said they were interrupted six times or more per hour. Work can and does call on us any hour of the day or night. The concept of weekends seems to have lost all meaning. We never have uninterrupted downtime.

If that weren't enough, we are constantly being flooded with information—from the Internet, magazines, TV, radio, books. We wonder why so many of us have short-term memory problems, why, in the words of Rick Wagonheim of R/Greenberg Associates, "we're all suffering from at least a little attention deficit disorder." Our poor brains are just crying out, "NO MORE!"

All this stimulation and outward attention has one effect: to make everything a blur and to create a sense of mental restlessness that is the antithesis of patience. David Shenk writes about this in *The End of Patience*: "As we go to higher info altitudes, where the information moves faster . . . our eyes, ears, and cerebral cortexes have more to keep up with. We do keep up, but in order to do so we habituate ourselves to shorter moments of concentration . . . and to a manic routine of 'multitasking' which so often leads to half-baked ideas and performance.

"And yes, we lose quiet moments, moments of reflection."

We don't just need time to reflect. We also need adequate sleep. The latest statistics on sleep patterns in the United States reveal that one in seven Americans suffers from insomnia on any given night, and one in ten of us has chronic sleep problems. The National Sleep

Foundation claims the average American is sleeping 20 percent less than a century ago, or one and a half fewer hours per night.

That hour and a half may seem like not such a big deal. But researchers are finding that it leads to all sorts of health problems including higher blood pressure and blood sugar levels, and has been identified as a factor in disasters such as Three-Mile Island, Chernobyl, the Exxon *Valdez*, and the *Challenger* space shuttle. Many of us are going around in a sleep-deprived state that is as dangerous as being drunk.

We all need enough sleep and we all need waking hours in which we are not accountable to anyone else. Otherwise we just won't have the mental and physical reserves life requires. Each of us needs to find our own way with this, schedule-wise. I work incredibly hard between the hours of eight and six. After that, I refuse to do business. And, with few exceptions, I do not work on weekends. As a consequence of these "rules," I find that I have much more patience. Conversely, when I have violated my rules for too long, everyone and everything drives me crazy.

Baseball legend Satchel Paige put it this way: "If your stomach disputes you, lie down and pacify it with cooling thoughts." Amen! Tune out as well as in and watch your patience soar.

WHAT DOES THIS MATTER IN THE

LARGER SCHEME OF THINGS?

> Keep cool: it will all be one a hundred years hence.
>
> *Ralph Waldo Emerson*

Last weekend was the Fourth of July and Ana was glued to my side for four straight days. "Mommy, can we go swimming now? . . . Mommy, Mommy, can I have juice? . . . Mommy, umm, umm, Mommy can we go swimming now? Mommy, can I watch *The Wiggles*? Mommy, Mommy, Mommy . . ." I lost count of how many times she said "mommy" at 1,372. Finally on Sunday night, I asked her if she would please go for ten minutes without asking me a question because I needed a break. Her response? "Why?" (Which, by the way, dissolved me into laughter, a great patience booster.)

Mostly I survived the experience without losing my temper by putting her behavior into a bit of perspective. In the big picture of our lives, what does The Four Days of Endless Questions matter? I reminded myself that I'm lucky that she wants my attention so much. Having raised teenagers, I know that the time when I'm the center of her universe, the object of her adoration, will be over in the blink of an eye and that I might as well savor it while I can.

When I set out to learn about something, I read every book on the subject and carefully study those I know who possess the quality I want in myself. I watch them in action; I ask a lot of questions. Books give me theory, but tend to be short on practice. In the case of patience, there is a lot out there about how we ought to be patient, but precious little on how we actually do it. So I've relied very heavily on people I know to teach me the ins and outs of this elusive quality.

One thing I've discovered is that, one way or another, like I did with Ana, patience is created by putting the irritant—person, place, or thing—into perspective. "I ask myself," said one friend, "whether this will matter in fifteen years or fifteen days. Or even fifteen minutes. Almost always that helps me see that whatever I think is worthy of getting worked up over is actually no big deal." Or as my friend Dawna, who has struggled with cancer on and off for thirty-some years, wrote in an email to me yesterday: "Well, a hundred things went wrong today, but they're all better than cancer!"

Whenever we put whatever is happening into a larger perspective, we automatically gain patience. That's because we take our focus off the particulars of the situation—that Jim didn't take out the trash, again; that Dad didn't thank us, again, for the visit—and place it in the larger context of the overall meaning of our lives.

From this wider place, we can ask some vital questions: Does this really matter? What *is* important here? Jim is a great father and a kind gentle mate. What's a bit of trash-forgetting in relation to that? What do we really want from our relationship? More love and a sense of togetherness or a cleaner house?

Patience is created when we keep our eyes on the big picture and don't get so caught up in the minutia of our daily lives. It's like having a wide-angle lens on a camera as well as a zoom. Up close, even a molehill can seem overwhelming; from a distance, we can see that in fact it's not a mountain. The good news is that you're holding the camera—and can switch lenses anytime you want.

PEOPLE ARE ONLY HUMAN

I love being married. It's so great to find that one special person
you want to annoy for the rest of your life.

Rita Rudner

Before I met my husband, I lived for fourteen years with a man
named Will. During the last six years of our relationship, he
worked an hour and a half away in a very high-powered job that required a lot of hours. I never knew when he'd be home. This was in
the days before cell phones, so I made what to me was a simple request: please call me at 5 P.M. every day to let me know when you'll
be leaving the office. That way I can plan for dinner, etc.

Easy, right? He couldn't do it, at least not consistently. He'd call
for days in a row and then forget. He'd get tied up in a meeting.
He'd get stuck on a plane. Whatever. I could not get him to do it.

The more he forgot, the angrier I became. Eventually my patience disappeared completely; every lapse was a reminder of all the times he had forgotten. He began to avoid me because all I was doing was complaining.

If there is one lesson I wish I learned before I was in my forties, it is that you can't control someone else's behavior. Honestly, you can't. People will be people. But so many of our communications at work and at home revolve around trying to get other people to behave differently. Our efforts may result in someone understanding a bit better what we want and why, but ultimately whether or not a person changes is entirely up to him or her. We can offer support, but we can't make the person dance to our tune.

I can't control whether my husband does his back exercises, although I can support him in doing them if he wants to; I can't control whether my employees are self-motivated, although I can create the conditions that would increase the likelihood of their taking responsibility; I couldn't even control when my then three-year-old would be potty trained, although I could encourage her.

This is such a blind spot for most of us that in *The Inner Game of Work*, Tim Gallwey offers a list of what we can and can't control in relation to other people. You can't control the other person's attitude or receptivity; how well he or she listens; the other person's motivation or priorities; his or her availability; whether he or she likes you; his or her ability to understand your point; how the other interprets what you have to say; whether the person accepts your point.

You can control your attitude toward the other person; your attitude toward learning; how receptively you listen; your acknowledgments of the person's point of view; your respect for the other person's time; your expression of enthusiasm for his or her idea; the amount of time you spend listening and speaking; your idea of yourself.

Notice the difference between the two lists. You can't control *anything* about someone else, but you have complete control of how you relate to him or her, and that, of course, will drastically impact his or her willingness to receive your viewpoint.

The more we recognize our complete lack of control over others, the more patience we'll have because we'll stop bashing our heads against the rock of the way they are and begin to aim our patience in the right direction—toward ourselves putting up with whatever it is that we want them to change.

In trying circumstances with other human beings, we can do no better than remember the Serenity Prayer: "God, grant me the serenity to accept the things I can't change, the courage to change the things I can, and the wisdom to know the difference."

SOME THINGS ARE WORTH

WAITING FOR

Waiting sharpens desire. In fact it helps us recognize
where our real desires lie. It separates our passing
enthusiasms from our true longings.

David Runcorn

A while ago, I read an article in the *New York Times* about the fact
that J. K. Rowling was having trouble finishing up book five in the
Harry Potter series and her young readers were losing patience.
One was even quoted as saying something like "If she doesn't
hurry, we're going to move on to caring about something else."

This remark really bothered me. Not because I know for sure
that the latest Harry Potter book is worth waiting for. But because
of the underlying attitude such a comment implies: you must immediately satisfy my desires or I'm out of here. If it were an isolated
comment by one individual, it would not have made such an

impression on me. But it reflects, I believe, a growing trend within society as a whole: we're too fickle to hang in there for something we say we want.

The irony is, say those who study such things, that when we do get everything we want as soon as we want it, we get jaded and dissatisfied with everything. It's the malaise of those who are born into extreme wealth—nothing ends up pleasing because it came too easily. There is something in the human psyche that needs to work toward what we desire in order to feel truly satisfied. Part of what feels good about getting what we want, it turns out, is that we've had to wait for it. Think of the taste of freshly baked bread after you've allowed the yeast to do its work. The wait sharpens your appetite.

I experienced the truth of this recently. A few years ago, I had to downsize due to economic realities, moving from a designer-built house with hardwood floors to a much smaller nondescript place with wall-to-wall beige carpeting that soon showed every stain a toddler and two cats could produce. I wanted to rip that carpet out from the day I laid eyes on it. So I saved my pennies and, four years later, my wish came true as I installed hardwood flooring throughout the house. Glistening golden tan oak with a smooth, shiny surface—my heart sings every time I cast my eyes on it. And, funny thing, I appreciate those floors much more than I did the ones in my previous house. Because I waited and worked for them.

When we recognize that waiting actually can bring greater

enjoyment than the immediate gratification of our needs, it makes patience much easier to practice. If I had known this, I could have said to myself as I stared at that disgusting carpet, Imagine how much more pleasure I'm going to have when I finally *do* get my floors!

Being made to wait has another benefit. It helps us figure out what we truly want and what really matters to us. I wanted those floors on day one and 1,460 days later I still wanted them. They were no passing fancy.

Remembering that some things are worth waiting for helps us decide what it is that is worth the wait, and to prize it truly when we do receive it.

IT WILL WORK OUT

Faith is belief in the unseen, the quietly held conviction
that even though you can't imagine how, at some time,
in some place, in the right way, the thing
you desire will indeed come to pass.

Daphne Rose Kingma

Sara is an entrepreneur in her late twenties who just opened a high-end business in a tough economy. "I find myself constantly irritable with my partner and my employees," she confessed to me. "My partner spends half the day saying 'chill out' to me. The worst part is that I think he's right. My impatience is not helping the situation, but I can't seem to snap out of it."

Sara has a great deal of self-awareness. When I asked her why she thought she was so impatient with everyone including herself, she got very quiet, and then said, "Oh, I see what it is, I'm afraid of the future. I'm so anxious about the possibility of failing that I am trying to do everything to keep the bad future from happening. Meanwhile my impatience is only increasing the chances that we will fail!"

As this young woman discovered, one of the attitudes that fosters patience is faith in a good outcome. When we believe in a happy future, we can wait more calmly now. This takes faith—in ourselves, our partners, our God, the benevolence of the universe—because we have no guarantee one way or another. We must live as if it will turn out, without knowing precisely how it will end up. And that is not always easy, particularly when there's a lot at stake.

The irony is that, while there are no guarantees, from the state of serenity that faith produces, it is more likely that the good outcome will occur. When we are fearful and impatient, we are off-balance, cut off from our deep inner wisdom which could guide us through the challenges we're facing. With our patience intact, we can apply all of our resources, both inner and outer, to the task at hand.

Faith in the good outcome doesn't mean that we become Pollyannas with our heads in the sand, oblivious to the real hardships of our lives. We should be prudent and seek quality advice and support when needed. We must tell ourselves the truth of our situation, even if it's not pretty. Then, armed with the facts and our faith, we can make the best decisions possible.

I once had a client who came to me and said, "I have two weeks until my business runs out of money. I have faith in my products and myself. What do you think I should do?" The two of us brainstormed for one hour and then she left. I didn't see her for six months. Then, out of the blue, I got a call from her saying that she had found a distributor and was hanging in there.

Faith in a good outcome doesn't guarantee that life will turn out exactly as we want it. Businesses and relationships fail; the stock market goes down as well as up. Ultimately our faith asks us to believe that even if it doesn't turn out the way we wanted, it still is for the best—we developed resources we never knew we had; formed friendships we wouldn't have otherwise; learned skills we can put to good use.

That's what Sara came to see—that even if her business failed, she would not have. She would have benefited immensely from the experience, particularly if she used it as an occasion to grow in patience, wisdom, and faith. And that alone would be a good outcome.

IT TAKES AS LONG AS IT TAKES

Some things can only happen through time.
They only happen—time carries them.

M. C. Richards

A few months ago, my husband lost his job when the company he was working for went out of business. Going to what he thought was an informational interview, he stumbled upon the perfect new opportunity—the place was close by, with flexible hours to accommodate our daughter's needs, good health insurance, in an industry he loves. The woman who spoke with him had just decided she needed help.

The two of them seemed to click, although she was making no promises. The job was with a large, public institution and there were many hoops to go through. It would take a month, she thought, before he would know one way or the other.

A month passed. He continued to look, but nothing fell into his lap. The woman called at one point to say that the process was still going on. After two months, he wondered whether he should issue her an ultimatum, but decided since this was a job he really wanted, he should wait patiently. Three months passed; he took a temporary position. Several more times he was tempted to call her up and read her the riot act, but decided that it was better to be upbeat and eager when they spoke. Finally, yesterday, all that patience paid off—four months to the day after his first interview, he was hired.

I believe he got that job because he remembered a crucial lesson: things take as long as they take. Or, as some spiritual teacher once said, "You can't push the river." I thought of this recently when someone shared her eighty-three-year-old grandmother's wisdom: "When you've got a cold, you can bundle up, stay in bed, drink chicken soup, and it will be gone in seven days. Or you can do nothing about it and it will be gone in seven days."

Maybe you're not suffering from a cold or waiting for a job, but chances are there are things in your life that you must simply wait for, even if you don't want to: to meet the right person; for the test results to come in; to make more money; to know whether your child will get the college scholarship. We're all being asked to wait seemingly beyond our limits.

When we remember that whatever it is that's driving us crazy is going to take as long as it takes to resolve, it's easier to be patient. We surrender to time as it passes through us, rather than insisting it happen now. A baby takes a full nine months to grow in the womb. We don't want it to arrive prematurely. What if we viewed the things we are trying to hurry along like new life instead? How would that affect our capacity to wait?

The more we reconcile ourselves to the fact that life moves at its own pace, the more patience we'll have. This kind of patience, which goes far beyond putting up with the momentary irritation of the laundry undone or someone interrupting you before you've finished speaking, is soul making. Waiting patiently asks us to allow life to move through and transform us as we bend like cattails in the wind, twisting and turning but somehow surviving.

THERE'S MORE THAN ONE

RIGHT WAY

Patience is something you admire in the driver
behind you, but not in the one ahead.

Bill Mcglashen

Don and I were in the car. He was driving. Coming up on a yellow
light, he stopped rather than accelerating. I sighed. You know the
kind of sigh I mean. The longtime couples' sigh that says, You are
trying my patience, but I am not going to argue. The light changed
and he took off, more slowly than I would have. I sighed again. He
pulled into a parking lot. "There's a space," I said, pointing to the
first one that appeared. He drove on, looking for one closer to our
destination. I sighed.

Later on, I thought about those sighs and the thousands of others I've made in the ten years we've been together. It's not enjoyable

to become impatient with the person you love. So why does it happen to me so often? Suddenly I had a flash of insight—it's because I believe there is a right way to do things. My way.

Inside of me is a Know-It-All who spends her time judging the people closest to me. And I'm not just talking about things worthy of being judged, like morality and ethics. I'm talking judging someone negatively for stopping at a yellow light because I determined there was time to get through! The loving part of me wants to say, "Oh please! Give the guy a break." But the Know-It-All has quite a hold on me when it comes to my spouse and she's one impatient lady. Things have to be done on her terms, on her timetable, or she gets annoyed.

I think Ms. Know-It-All has a lot of company. Much of our intolerance and anger come from believing that we have the corner on the right way to be, and the rest of the world is wrong for not marching to our tune.

Recently I came across a synonym for patience I'd never heard before: "sweet reasonableness." I loved that! It reminds me that when we're reasonable, we can see that there are many ways to get things done. The people in our lives are different from us, thank goodness, and so of course they will go about doing things differently. Differently, not better or worse. The less time we spend judging them, the happier we'll be. Plus we empower the people in our lives when we trust them to do something in their own way and at their rhythm. We signal that we know they are capable and appreciate their competency.

However, my judgmental part is very strong; I've spent a lot of time feeding it. I've begun dealing with it by forming a club with a friend with a similar streak. We call it the Know-It-All Club. We talk to each other when we're on our high horses about our spouses and help the other person to see sweet reason.

I also take inspiration from the wise counsel of a woman known as Peace Pilgrim who once wrote, "Judging others will avail you nothing and injure you spiritually. Only if you inspire others to judge themselves will anything worthwhile have been accomplished."

But the most useful thing I've found is to ask myself in those moments, Who appointed you God? That reminds me that I am not infallible and, in remembering that, I am able to dance more gracefully with my partner in the give-and-take that is a truly loving relationship.

WELCOME, TEACHERS

OF PATIENCE

To practice patience, you need a real rascal to help you.
It's no use practicing on gentle and kind creatures,
for they require no patience.

from "The Magic of Patience,"
a Jataka tale written around 300 B.C.

My good friend Kate has a troublesome sister. They have never gotten along, from the day Kate was born, nine years after her sister Ruth. The two of us were discussing our sisters one day when Kate said something startling.

"Ruth was incredibly jealous of me because I stole her only-child status," explained Kate, "and even though it's fifty years later, there's still tension. I can moan and complain that I don't have a good relationship with my sister, but ultimately, I give thanks for her because she is my greatest teacher. Whatever patience I possess, I got from dealing with her. It's important to me to have as good a relationship as possible with her, so I've learned to put up with her coolness and to give without expectation of kindness in return."

What an incredible attitude, I thought. To be able to welcome into our lives those who are the most trying to us because they will teach us patience.

I was reminded of Kate's comment recently when I told a client of mine that I was writing a book on patience. He has a teenage daughter, Tina, who has had serious learning issues since birth. "You know," he said, "I always used to pray for patience. And then God answered my prayers—he sent me Tina! And boy did I have to learn patience."

What Kate and my client taught me is that when we see those who challenge us as teachers rather than burdens, our patience instantly grows. We don't have to grit our teeth and simply bear it; we're learning something of value. We're learning how to love, to open our hearts, to grow beyond our previous limitations. This perspective makes life easier to go through. Rather than resisting what is happening to us, we use it as fodder to become wiser and kinder, rather than bitter or mean-spirited.

There is a Tibetan teaching story that goes something like this: A monk was meditating by himself in a cave high in the mountains. One day a herdsman came back and, intrigued, asked the monk, "What are you doing here all by yourself?" "Meditating on patience," replied the monk. The herdsman, turning to leave, shouted in response, "Well, you can just go to hell." "Oh yeah," the monk yelled back, "*You* go to hell!" The herdsman laughed all the way down the mountain.

As this story illustrates, cultivating patience is meaningless unless we can use it when we need it. The herdsman was a great teacher, for he showed the monk his understanding was only intellectual. If the monk could see this teacher in that light, he would finally be truly on his way.

By opening our hearts to the people and things that challenge us, we become spiritually and emotionally supple, less prone to being knocked over by whatever curves life throws at us. Difficult people and events become interesting opportunities for further growth, rather than threatening obstacle courses we must endure. From this place, we actually can enjoy life more, whatever is happening.

THERE'S A TIME TO WAIT AND
A TIME TO PEDAL LIKE MAD

If there is a defining characteristic of a man
as opposed to a boy, maybe it's patience.

Lance Armstrong

Lance Armstrong is inarguably one of the greatest cyclists ever to jump on a bike. Physiologically he is perfectly suited to the sport: his heart is much larger than average, which allows him to pump more oxygen faster than competitors. He has grit, determination, the capacity to withstand enormous physical discomfort. But, as he relates in *It's Not About the Bike*, he could not win the most important bike race in the world, the three-week Tour de France, until he learned to wait.

"My reputation was as a single-day racer: show me the start line and I would win on adrenaline and anger, chopping off my competitors one by one. . . . If you raced that way in the Tour, you would drop out after two days. It required a longer view. The Tour was a matter of mustering the right resources at the right times, of patiently feeding out your strength at the necessary level, with no wasted motion or energy."

Lance raced competitively in Europe for almost five years before he began to learn how to wait. His coach lectured him over and over to hold back; he "would ride smart for a while and then backslide. I just couldn't get it through my head that in order to win I had to ride more slowly at first. It took some time to reconcile myself to the notion that being patient was different than being weak."

Then he got testicular cancer and almost died. And while he fought the disease as aggressively as he rode, the experience matured him. He learned the value of waiting. And he went on win the Tour de France—four times so far.

Like the younger Lance Armstrong, one thing that has always scared me about patience is worrying about when it falls over into passivity. When is waiting just the right thing and when is it a cop-out? When am I being appropriately patient and when am I just allowing someone else to run over me?

People who I admire for their patience seem to understand timing; they know that there's a time to wait and a time to act, and they trust themselves to know which is which. Each of us has a natural tendency toward either hurrying up or waiting, which we gravitate to unless we pay attention. Lance's youthful inclination was to pedal harder, and then lack the energy for the long haul. Someone else might have waited too long, and missed the opportunity to surge ahead of the pack.

There is no great Patience Judge in the sky who can tell us precisely what is the right amount of time to wait on anyone or anything. But when we remember that there is a time to wait and a time to put the pedal to the metal, it creates a resting point where all of our intelligence—our intuition as well as our rationality—can come to the fore.

Patience is very much about developing trust in our sense of timing. "Patience and timing are inextricably linked," writes Barry Boyce in an article in the *Shambhala Sun*. "Patience, which we can regard with such excruciation, offers a hidden reward. When we stop watching the pot, we may learn that it boils right on time."

ENOUGH IS ENOUGH

Folks differs, dearie. They differs a lot. Some can stand things
that others can't. There's never no way of knowin'
how much they can stand.

Ann Petry

In the past two years, I had a most dramatic experience with patience. I had decided to sell my publishing business. Along came a
potential buyer who was very interested. If he bought, I would have
been well off for the rest of my life. If he didn't, the business might
have had to declare bankruptcy.

He moved incredibly slowly, but he did move forward. Every so
often, I would call and see if I could speed things up, and he would
assure me he was moving as fast as he could. I didn't have another
buyer at that point; all the others had disappeared when we accepted this person's contingency offer. All I could do, for nine

agonizing months, was wait until he finished the examination process and made up his mind.

Often I would wake in the middle of the night and think, I may go bankrupt or I may never have to worry about money again. Poised between potential disaster and great gain, it seemed the best choice to wait.

One of my problems with patience is that I am afraid my waiting button is out of whack. Some things I am willing to wait years for, others not even seconds. I'm not even sure what criteria I am using to judge whether patience is appropriate. But I do know this—there are many situations when you should say, "Enough. I will wait no longer." As in, for example, "I won't wait any longer for you to stop drinking. I would rather leave you than watch you kill yourself." Or "I will not put up with that person's physical and verbal abuse one more minute." Or "We have been meeting for months now without moving forward. I think it's time to give up this business idea."

However, as Ann Petry suggests in the above quote, I can't tell you what the point is for you because I am not you. I can't even necessarily know for myself what that point is on an absolute scale because it varies with the situation. I do know that it is crucial for the practice of patience to know when to stop being patient. Only you can know that moment.

Sometimes, I set a deadline in my mind in advance: I will do this for six months and then reevaluate. I have a business associate who has a three-meeting rule: if no forward movement has happened in three meetings, she's out of there. Other times, I use a bitterness indicator. If I've begun to be resentful, maybe it's time for me to say "no more."

But because so many situations call for patience beyond what we imagined, this is very tricky territory. Maybe we were being called on to wait just one more day, one more week, to try just one more thing. Books (like this one!) are full of stories of people who hung in there beyond all reasonableness and finally succeeded.

That's why only you can judge for yourself in the quiet counsel of your own deepest wisdom. And you need to know your outer limits.

I recently read a joke that captured this idea in a lighthearted way. An elderly couple has filed for divorce. The judge turns to them and says, "You mean to tell me that you are willing to throw in the towel after sixty-five years of marriage?" The wife turns to the judge and responds, "Your honor, enough is enough."

The end of my dramatic waiting story? The man did not purchase my business. Eventually someone else did and I ended up neither bankrupt nor rich. But I learned a great deal about what patience feels like. And I feel much better equipped to pull the patience plug if need be.

BE HERE NOW

Every moment a beginning.
Every moment an end.

Mark Salzman

Eckhart Tolle is a spiritual teacher who, in his youth, lived with intense anxiety and depression; often he considered suicide. Then, on his twenty-ninth birthday, he had a spontaneous enlightenment experience, which left him with a profound "undercurrent of peace" that remains to this day, thirteen years later. What he experienced, he says, is the "power of now."

"Realize deeply that the present moment is all you ever have," he writes in his best-selling book, *The Power of Now.* Whatever pain or conflict we feel is "always some form of non-acceptance, some form of resistance to what is. . . . You don't want what you've got, and you want what you haven't got." When you come into the present moment as it truly is, there are no problems, "only situations—to be dealt with now, or left alone and accepted as part of the 'isness' of the present moment until they change or *can* be dealt with."

Tolle's words have profound implications for patience seekers. Think about a recent occasion when you lost your patience. Was it because a certain something was happening yet again? Again he leaves the room in the middle of your sentence. Again she forgets to pay the bills. Again you are left to clean up the mess.

Or was it in some way a fear about the future, perhaps that you wouldn't get a project done on time or that your dreams would never come to fruition? Either way your loss of patience represented a stepping out of the present and either fretting about the past or worrying about the future.

That's why one of the best attitudes to hold, when it comes to patience, is present moment awareness. Here I am in this moment. This moment, this one that has never happened before and will never come again. Impatience is always about the past (This has happened too many times before) or the future (When will what I want to happen happen?). Being in the present is about the now, where what is simply is.

When we are truly in the present moment, we do not worry. There is nothing to strain toward or away from. We just are—in a line of cars on a rainy Sunday, hearing the buzz of a plane overhead. Sitting in front of a computer reading emails. Cooking dinner.

Patience is the willingness to be in the now exactly as it is. Even if we wish or hope or pray that someday it will change, patience allows us to live as happily and contentedly as possible right now.

That seems easy to do when life is going well. But it is also the secret to surviving adversity. The courageous Protestant theologian Dietrich Bonhoeffer understood this. In *Letters and Papers from Prison*, composed while he was held captive by the Nazis, he wrote: "It is the mark of a grown-up man, as compared with a callow youth, that he finds his center of gravity wherever he happens to be at the moment."

Each of us has our own way of coming to this moment. In Aldous Huxley's novel *Island*, brightly colored parrots are taught to continuously croak, "Attention. Here and Now. Attention. Here and Now," to help islanders remember.

Short of a talking parrot, you can try a simple technique of Thich Nhat Hanh's. As you breathe, say to yourself: Breathing in, I am aware of breathing in. Breathing out, I am aware of breathing out. You'll be amazed at how calm and patient you'll feel in seconds flat. From this calm place, we are more prepared to greet life as it unfolds, moment by moment.

4.

THE PRACTICES OF PATIENCE

The shortest and surest way to live with honor in the world is to be
in reality what we would appear to be; all human virtues
increase and strengthen themselves by the
practice and experience of them.

Socrates

Ultimately our task as patience seekers is to increase self-awareness.
New brain research suggests that the time between an impulse and
a response is half a second. Awareness increases that time by
another half second. In other words, awareness doubles the time
between impulse and action. That half second is the space in which
patience is a viable option. Without that pause, we're operating

from the emotional part of our brains that cares only that we get what we want right this minute, whether or not that's ultimately the most beneficial thing.

To that end, the practices suggested here all help increase your awareness and thus, your options. At first, this is a very conscious process in which we notice our impulse to respond in our habitual hurried way and then opt for patience instead. The more we practice, however, the more patience becomes automatic, until we choose it without even being aware of the choice.

TELL YOURSELF THE TRUTH ABOUT
WHERE YOU ARE RIGHT NOW

Something happens when we don't resist, when we don't hate
ourselves for what we are experiencing. Our hearts open . . .

Sharon Salzberg

A couple years ago, I came across Robert Fritz's book *The Path
of Least Resistance*. Fritz's work is about conscious change: how
people and organizations change on purpose. His idea, based on
the laws of physics, is very simple. We begin by telling ourselves
the truth about what we want and where we are right now in
relation to what we want, without judgment or criticism. So to begin to cultivate more patience, we first must ask how patient we
already are.

Fritz believes it's not useful to just say you want "more" patience, because what is more? How will you measure it? In order to know where you are and where you want to be, you need some way of quantifying. Since patience is not something you either have or don't have, but rather is a quality you exhibit more or less of at any given time, we can usefully measure it on a scale from -5 to +5, with -5 being the least patient you can be and +5 being the most.

Think of your own life. What behaviors and feelings would be a -5 to you? What behaviors and feelings would a +5 be? A -5 for me would be throwing something or saying something really mean to someone else. It would feel like a raging red storm I had no control over. A +5 would be feeling totally calm in my body when Ana is dawdling and I must drop her at school and be in a meeting in twenty minutes but I take time to receive what she is saying.

Now, given those two self-created measurements, where on average would you like to be and where do you spend most of your time? For me, I'd say I'd really like to be at 4.5 and I probably am at 2.

When we tell ourselves the truth about where we are and where we want to be, we realize there is a gap between the two. That gap, says Fritz, is a good thing. He calls it creative tension, because it allows something new to be born by causing energy to move from current reality to your desired result. You don't even need to worry about exactly *how* it will happen, says Fritz. Tell yourself the truth about current reality (without berating yourself), keep your goal in front of you as you try some things, and notice what happens.

Try it and see. Come up with your two numbers and write them down. Experiment with the practices in this section that you feel drawn to. Then check in again in a month (it takes time for this to work). What are your two numbers now?

TUNE IN TO YOURSELF

IN THE MORNING

It's taken time and practice . . . to appreciate that how [we] start
the day sets the pace for everything that comes next.

Tracy D. Sarriugarte and
Peggy Rowe Ward

I have a friend who is a preschool teacher. One day she shared with
me one of her great parenting secrets: "Spend twenty minutes first
thing in the morning with your child with no agenda and the rest
of the day will go much more smoothly. You'll have less trouble getting ready for school, less clinging when you drop your child off,
and fewer conflicts at the end of the day." I took her advice and it
was remarkably effective. When I reported back in, she told me
that I would be amazed at how many parents tell her they don't
have twenty minutes to spend, and so they end up struggling with

their kids all day and evening long, using up way more time than twenty minutes.

To me, this is a story about how we can so easily be penny-wise and pound-foolish, with time as well as money. It's also about how setting the tone in the morning really does affect what happens for the rest of the day. Many people, particularly women, report to me that when they take even ten minutes for themselves when they first wake up, they have much more resilience the rest of the day. Kids, coworkers, spouses—all feel a little less overwhelming when they have taken just a few precious minutes to tune in to themselves first.

That's because part of our lack of patience comes from the fact that we are being pulled in so many directions that we don't have time to pay attention to ourselves. No wonder we're short-tempered with everyone else—we're shortchanging ourselves!

Right now, take a few moments to figure out when and where you can find the time to tune in to yourself in the morning. I tend to wake up before Don and Ana, and I relish that time lying in bed when there are no demands on me. But you can also take ten minutes in the parking lot before heading into the office, or at the school when you drop your child off.

Those few minutes are your chance to prepare yourself for the day ahead. How are you feeling? What's on your mind? What is your soul longing for? Where might you need some help? What quality do you want to bring into your day—a sense of spacious-ness, peace of mind, an open heart?

Then for one minute in the evening, mentally review the day, noticing whether your morning tune-in was effective. Were you more resilient and flexible? Did you cruise through the day in a generally positive way? What worked and didn't? Learning happens after an event when we stop and reflect, so give yourself that one minute in the evening to figure out whether the tune-in is useful or not.

Try it for a week and then decide whether this is something you would like to do on a regular basis. Our reservoir of patience is refilled through attention to our own needs.

WHEN AM I PATIENT?

LET ME COUNT THE WAYS

You must first have a lot of patience
to learn to have patience.

Stanislaw J. Lec

When we adopted Ana from China, she was one year old and seriously neglected. She couldn't even roll from front to back, weighed only fourteen pounds, and had second-degree burns on her buttocks from lying in urine. As soon as I laid my eyes on this beautiful child who had been allowed to languish for thirteen months, all my maternal instincts went into overdrive. I made a decision: this precious being simply needed love and attention to flourish.

From that moment on, I had all the patience I needed. I refused to look at development charts in the pediatrician's office that described where she should be. I refused to compare her height and weight to children of the same age. When she began stuttering at age three, I refused to draw attention to the problem, allowing her the time to work it out on her own.

Don and I held her, slept with her until she was four, and, aside from the time she was in preschool, spent virtually every waking hour with her. Today, at five and a half, she is a bright, beautiful, articulate, hula-hooping champion who is about to enter the advanced kindergarten at her school.

Ana is proof that love can conquer all, but she is also a clue to where my patience easily resides. I have tremendous patience with people. I can get occasionally frustrated, annoyed, or even angry, but ultimately my patience kicks back in. I simply refuse to give up on a living being who has come into my sphere.

You too have enormous patience for something and the more you study what fosters your patience, the more you will be able to engage it in any circumstance. Here's a way to begin. Take a few minutes to make a list of when you are naturally patient. Is it with people? With adults and children, or one more than the other? With animals? Or, like my daughter, in making things with your hands? Do you persist until you meet your goal, no matter what? Where and how does your patience exhibit itself?

Now look at your list and study your pattern of success. Think about what makes patience possible for you during those times, when it's easy. You probably aren't consciously aware of it, but you are actually doing something to trigger your patience. It could be a feeling you have, a picture you see in your head, a phrase you tell yourself. You are doing something that allows you to hang in there.

When Bob, a client, did this exercise, he discovered that he is very patient with breakdowns of all kinds in systems at work because he sees a picture of himself succeeding in the past and that gives him confidence in the current situation. With me, whenever I'm patient, it's because I've felt my deep desire to foster the growth of another living being. When I feel that feeling, my patience is virtually endless.

Once you discover your pattern of success, you can use it in situations that normally try your patience. For instance, I now engage my patience better when I'm waiting by framing the experience as an opportunity to foster my own growth. When dealing with his kids, which is where Bob often lost his patience, he began bringing to mind a picture of a happy outcome as soon as his blood began to boil. As a consequence, he didn't lose his patience at home nearly as often.

You are patient. By seeing where and how, you can learn to access your patience when you need it most.

KNOW YOUR IMPATIENCE TRIGGERS

Patience . . . is cultivated through the rational process of analysis. . . .
It is essential that we begin our training in patience calmly,
not while experiencing anger.

the Dalai Lama

My father was a mild-mannered soul. Most of the time, that is. And I was a good kid, who only wanted to please him. Most of the time, I did. But every once in a while, he would lose all patience with me. He'd grit his teeth and his jaw would bulge and he would speak to me in a low growl. My terrible offense? Brushing my teeth outside of the bathroom!

I was reminded of that the other day when the mother of a friend of Ana's told me that mornings were the worst time for her when it came to being patient with her three kids. "I don't know why," she confided, "perhaps it's the pressure to get everyone out the door on time, but I lose it almost every morning."

That got me thinking about when I lose patience most easily. Waiting in line immediately pops to mind. But the other danger zones for me are mechanical objects. The person who came up with the phrase "all thumbs" had me in mind when he or she coined the term. Doing anything with my hands is incredibly challenging. This has always been true. When I had to learn to sew in home ec in junior high, my sister would leave the house when she saw the sewing machine being hauled out.

Even now, I embody the term "helpless female" when it comes to anything that requires hand-eye coordination or mechanical ability. When I cook, which I love to do, I veto any recipe that requires too much intricate rolling or stuffing or I'm likely to end up throwing a chicken breast across the kitchen.

What are your impatience triggers? They are different for each of us. For my mother, it's visual chaos: piles of toys left around, clothes on the floor, unmade beds. For my husband, it's being interrupted by Ana when he's trying to tell me something. For my friend Debra, it's voice mail loops where you can't ever get to a real person. Right now, take a couple minutes to note, in writing or in your mind, when and where you tend to be the most impatient.

When we bring to our awareness exactly what it is that causes us to "lose it," we increase our options of response. But only if we do not judge ourselves. If we tell ourselves that we are bad for being impatient when someone is speaking slowly, or for snapping at our kids, we will not change. In fact, there's a boomerang effect in which the behavior gets more firmly entrenched: we do it, then we beat ourselves up for doing it, then we do it even more. But if we can bring curiosity to our noticing—Oh, I really do go nuts every morning, isn't that interesting; I wonder what I can do about that—we can come up with better alternatives.

Take a look at your list. Is there something you can do to work around what's hardest for you? Or if it's unavoidable, can you offer yourself compassion for how hard it is? I once heard someone say, "I'm doing as good a job at this as I can now. If I could do better, I would." What loving self-talk; she told herself the truth, and acknowledged she wanted to improve, all without bashing herself!

As for me and my bumbling, I've learned to unabashedly pass things over to my husband or, increasingly, my very handy five-year-old. When I must do something mechanical on my own, I remind myself that this is difficult for me, and therefore gain a bit more patience with the situation. And I haven't been near a sewing machine in thirty-five years.

LEARN YOUR EARLY-WARNING SIGNS

Problems are only opportunities in work clothes.

Henry J. Kaiser

I was on the phone with Cynthia. She was talking about how she seems to go along just fine and then suddenly, out of nowhere, she loses her patience. "One minute I'm fine and the next, I am a harridan. I seem to get no warning I'm about to blow," she lamented.

Impatience often feels like that, a sudden summer squall that comes up out of nowhere in the midst of a peaceful sky-blue day. Once we lose it, there's not a whole lot to do except try to inflict as little damage as possible, and treat ourselves and those around us as kindly as possible after the fact. (Apologies work well too.)

But there are indicators that we are about to blow, we're just not aware of them. Sports psychologist Gary Mack calls them early-warning signs, like the red indicator lights on your car. It's really *not* happening out of the blue, although it may feel that way. We're doing something to tip ourselves in that direction.

For some of us, it might be something we say to ourselves, like, I can't stand this anymore. For others, it may be a scary picture of getting hurt. For still others, it is the feeling of holding our breath or of our heart racing.

Step one is to begin to notice what your sign is. For me, it's definitely a phrase in my head, something like, I'm not going to put up with this anymore. For you it might be completely different. Be gentle with yourself as you explore. You are bringing to awareness something that is operating below your level of ordinary attention. The best way to explore is, after an impatience episode, to track back to what happened inside you just before you lost it.

Once you discover your early-warning sign, try the second step. Do something different. Stand up or begin to doodle. Sing a silly song in your head. When you interrupt the program that usually runs you from patience to impatience, you increase the possibility of remaining calm.

When Cynthia tried this, at first she couldn't identify her early-warning sign. But by paying close attention a few times, she realized that she made a scary movie in her mind just before she snapped. She started singing to herself "You Are My Sunshine" when the movie started. It worked!

Study your early-warning signs and try something different the next time the "red light" comes on. That way the squalls of impatience won't take you by surprise. They might just roll out to sea without you.

TAKE A BREATHER

Nothing is more effective than a deep, slow inhale and release for
surrendering what you can't control and focusing again
on what is right in front of you.

Oprah Winfrey

Gary Mack works with professional athletes, helping them to maximize their performance. In his book, *Mind Gym*, he, like Oprah Winfrey, touts the power of conscious breathing to focus and calm the mind. To make this real, he first puts athletes through what he calls the "breathless exercise."

"First I tell the group that this is a contest. I am going to watch each of them and judge everyone's performance carefully. Then I begin barking verbal commands. 'Look left . . . look right . . . look left . . . look right, look right . . . look right . . .' As they continue the task, their anxiety increases. Their breathing pattern changes.

Without realizing it, many hold their breath." He then goes on to teach them to breathe consciously under stress.

I don't know about you, but much of my life seems like Mack's breathless exercise: look here, no here, no here. Constantly attending, constantly trying to keep up. Could something as easy as taking a few breaths boost my patience and increase my peace of mind? The answer, I've discovered, is yes. A few breaths, or more accurately, a few conscious breaths, since we are breathing all the time, gives us a split second to recall what's really important in the situation, rather than just reacting on impulse.

Breathing with awareness also helps us tune in to our bodies and notice what is going on internally. Patience and impatience are not just ideas in our minds, but also sensations in our bodies. We each have our own words for those sensations. To me, patience is a feeling of calm groundedness, a rooted, expansive feeling of well-being, while impatience is a jittery, flustered, off-balance sensation.

When we become aware of the sensation of impatience in our bodies, we can use our breath to come back to patience by slowing the inhales and exhales a bit. This signals our nervous system to begin the relaxation response. In as little as a minute, our shoulders relax, muscles loosen, blood pressure drops, and our heart beats a bit slower. From this physically calmer place, we are able to respond more effectively because we have access to all of our emotional and mental resources.

There are many ways to do calming breathing. In a stress-reduction report issued by the Harvard Medical School, there is a technique that can be done in less than a minute. It is particularly effective because it combines breathing with touch, which has also been found to be soothing.

Put one hand on your belly, just under your belly button. Breathe in, feeling your abdomen inflate. Hold for the count of three, then breathe out, feeling your abdomen deflate. Hold for the count of three. Repeat until you feel calmer.

You can use this technique anywhere, anytime—under the pressure of a deadline when your computer suddenly goes on the blink; when the kids are rubbing on your last nerve; when you're worried about getting somewhere on time. You can encourage your family and friends to do it when their patience wears thin as well.

I can't encourage you enough to try this patience formula. It is simply the best way we humans have of regrouping quickly. As Thich Nhat Hanh promises, "It needs only one conscious breath to be back in contact with yourself and everything around you, and three conscious breaths to maintain that contact." No matter how busy we are, we all have time for that!

CLIMB DOWN TO THE

BASE OF THE TREE

When the crowded refugee boats met with storms or pirates,
if everyone panicked, all would be lost. But if even one
person remained calm and centered, it was enough.
They showed the way for everyone to survive.

Thich Nhat Hanh

Buddhist monk Thich Nhat Hanh is from Vietnam. In his young adulthood, virtually everyone he loved in his country—his family, his fellow monks, the children in the orphanages he founded—died in the war. Yet he is one of the most peaceful and happy human beings you could ever come across. That's because, he says, peace can be found in every moment, even when life seems the most challenging.

One of the best ways to find peace is to get out of your head and into your body. Hanh likens it to being a tree in a strong storm. If the wind is raging and you are at the top of the tree, you will be tossed around violently. Climb down to the sturdy trunk and you will barely feel any movement whatsoever.

How do you get to the base of the tree? One way is by centering. Like mindful breathing, centering is a physical way of being fully present in the moment, with mind and body in harmony. From that place of rooted calmness, you are much better able to cope patiently with whatever is going on outside you, even if pirates are boarding your boat.

Centering, the base practice in the martial art of Aikido, has been one of the most useful techniques I've learned in cultivating patience. Here's the most dramatic example. From the first night we adopted Ana, she would awaken each evening, screaming. Once, twice, five times a night for almost four years, she would wake, hysterically crying and kicking, for as long as fifteen minutes at a time. She wasn't really awake; experts call the phenomenon night terrors.

In Ana's case, I believe they were a result of her abandonment as an infant. There was nothing we could do except hold her and tell her she was safe until she fell back into sound sleep. As she got bigger, it became impossible to hold her because her thrashing was so strong. All Don and I could do was sit next to her, tell her she was safe, and not abandon her again.

As any parent knows, as any compassionate person knows, it's very hard to watch a person in obvious agony and do nothing. In the beginning, I would get very agitated by just sitting. Then one day, I remembered I could center.

It was remarkably effective. I was able to stay fully present with her for as long as it took for her to calm down, without losing my patience, night after night, month after month, until she no longer woke up.

It worked for other things as well. I used it when she hit her terrible twos and would throw herself on the ground in a tantrum. I would center and say, "I see you are really frustrated. I am sorry you're so upset" without losing my cool. Because I was able to be present without getting caught up in her attempts to manipulate me, her tantrums soon stopped.

Now I use it any time someone comes at me with strong energy—frustration, upset, fear. It's automatic. I feel myself centering and from that place am able to respond in a way that is healthier for me and the other person.

So how do you center? I do it by bringing attention to my belly and imagine myself encircled by a sphere of energy about a handspan away from my body, including under my feet. Some people center by remembering what really matters to them, others by imagining their golf stance. Women sometimes think of their wombs. Anything that brings your center of gravity to your belly works.

To practice, try one of the techniques described above. Then, when you are ready, have someone gently push you on your shoulder and try to knock you over. If you are off-center, a gentle push will cause you to move. If you're centered, you are virtually immovable.

Center is not a place you find once and for all. You—and I—will find and lose it over and over again. But the more we practice, the easier it will be to find and the more instinctive it will be in times of need. Practice when you don't need to, with a willing but not too aggressive partner. The idea is not for you to land on the floor, but to get a sense of the feeling of centering.

After doing it a dozen times or so till it feels right (you'll know), try it when you feel your thermostat rising. Are you more patient and effective when you center? What helps you to do it? What helps you to remember to try it when your patience starts to fray?

Firmly rooted in the base of the tree of your being, you are much better able to cope with the storms that others bring your way.

ROAD SAGE, NOT ROAD RAGE

He who is slow to anger is better than the mighty.
And he who rules his spirit, than he who takes a city.

Proverbs 16:32

In her audiotape *Road Sage*, Sylvia Boorstein tells of a limo driver with whom she was once caught in a traffic jam on the way to an appearance on a live TV program. He worked for the station and so knew how important it was to get her there on time. But he never lost his composure, even though they were barely moving. And he did get her there on time. When she asked him about his capacity to be at ease despite the nerve-racking circumstances he found himself in each day, he explained, "What I'm doing could be a headache for me if I let it be."

This driver knew something that many of us need to remember:

we have a choice in how we respond to the situations we find ourselves in. For most of us, those circumstances involve huge amounts of time on clogged highways and byways. Each day, like the wise limo driver, we have a choice to panic over being late and get furious at other drivers, or relax and enjoy the ride, slow as it is.

More and more frequently, we are choosing the former option. The American Automobile Association (AAA) reports that aggressive driving is a factor in two-thirds of all accidents, while the California Highway Patrol reports that, in the San Francisco Bay Area, they receive four or five road rage complaints per hour during the commuting period.

It's not that people don't have provocation; there is a direct relationship between how crowded the road is and how aggressive drivers become. But there's another reason why road rage is so prevalent: it's an anonymous way to get our frustration out about other things. You know the old cartoon where the guy comes in from a hard day at work and yells at his wife, who yells at the kids, who kick the dog? The psychological term is "displacement." Rather than letting out your feelings at the person or situation that is actually troubling you, you vent on someone "safer."

Whatever the reasons, because we spend so much time in cars, commuting is the perfect time to practice patience. Patience means we don't cause accidents by weaving in and out of traffic, following too closely, or cutting other vehicles off. And when other drivers do behave badly toward us, patience lets us avoid a confrontation that could lead to no good.

Whether an aggressive driver or simply a line of unmoving cars is confronting you, it helps to consciously relax your body, particularly your hands on the steering wheel. Look around at the scenery, find a great station on the radio, listen to books on tape.

I always have to remind myself that I can live through being late because I tend to go into a tizzy about not being punctual. I got some help in that regard once when I was an hour late to a lawyer who charged $350 per hour. The whole drive I fretted about the money and what he would think of me. When I got there, he told me that the initial consultation was free and that my being late allowed him to get some needed work done. Now when I'm running late, I reassure myself by hoping for that kind of response again.

Notice the difference it makes in your trip and in how you feel when you arrive when you decide to play it cool.

ISSUE A STORM WARNING
TO CHILDREN

Me: "Ana, I'm losing my patience."
Ana (age three): "Don't worry Mama, I still have some."

I don't know about you, but one of the most difficult things for me about being a child was that I would be going along my merry way when all of a sudden, the adult in charge would be furious with me, and I would be yelled at, spanked, or sent to my room without any warning that I had exceeded the patience zone. Enduring my punishment, I vowed that I would never treat a child of mine that way. And I haven't.

All through the years I helped raise my two stepkids (who are now adults) and now with Ana, I've always issued a warning when my patience was being tested. That way, they know what's coming and can choose either to alter their behavior or endure my impatience. But it is their choice. They never experience my impatience or anger out of the blue. There's an early-warning system in place.

The system has worked remarkably well for twenty-five years. The kids always took the warning to heart and modified their behavior, and I did not have to become the Wicked Witch of the West, suffering self-loathing and remorse later.

Issuing a storm warning provides great protection for the little ones entrusted to you. But it also is useful for us parents. Sometimes, just hearing ourselves say out loud that we are at the end of the rope gives us the strength to carry on. If not, at least we end up respecting ourselves more because we've paused to give the warning before letting loose. When we give notice before acting, we prove to ourselves that we are emotionally trustworthy. We're worthy of the love that our children offer us, as well as our own high regard.

Try issuing a storm warning next time you feel an impatience hurricane coming on and notice what it does for you and yours. If you have trouble knowing when the storm is about to hit, try the practice called Learn Your Early-Warning Signs first (see page 139). And have compassion for yourself when you blow it.

TAP INTO YOUR INNER WISDOM

You have to leave the city of your comfort and go into the wilderness of
your intuition. What you'll discover will be wonderful.
What you'll discover will be yourself.

Alan Alda

When their kids graduated from college, Mark and Betty decided
to downsize from their large suburban home and move to the city.
They looked for months, until one day, Betty found her dream
condo. She'd wanted to live on this particular block her whole adult
life. They immediately placed a bid and went about selling the family homestead. But their house would not sell and they lost the
new place.

"At first," said Betty, "I was heartbroken and figured that I had
to find another option. But then a strange thing happened. From
somewhere inside of me came a message: Don't give up. This is

where you are supposed to live. It was weird because the condo was now gone. But something inside me told me to hang on. For a year I passed by it on my way to work and the thought would come again: Keep waiting. Then, one day, out of the blue, it went on sale again. This time, we were able to sell our house. And now here we are."

What Betty heard, I believe, was the voice of her intuition. We each have this deep, patient knowing that can help us when we are struggling. Is this a situation where we keep on pushing or is it better to give up? Should we do nothing or jump into action? Our internal wisdom can guide us.

It's great to hear the voice of our intuition as loudly as Betty did. But that doesn't usually happen. We have to get to our inner Wise One in other ways. In her book *Stirring the Waters*, Janell Moon offers a journal practice she calls "dialoguing" that can help.

Before you give it a try, please understand that journaling does not require writing in a blank book in neat rows. It doesn't even mean you have to write something down. You can do it as a series of ideas in balloons on a big piece of paper in no apparent order. You can read the following description and hold the questions in your head as you go for a walk, and notice what comes up for you. Depending on how your mind works, one method may be more effective than another. Give yourself permission to do what's right for you, not what you've been taught is the "right" way to journal.

First, write down or bring to mind the ten wisest people you know. Next, write down or bring to mind "a concern about your own patience," writes Moon. She continues:

> Maybe you're wondering if you should stay in a relationship. Or maybe you are in conflict with a friend and are trying to figure out the wisest, most loving response. All you need is something that you want counsel about patience on.

Now, consult your list of wise people and see which one could help you with this particular concern. Imagine a conversation with this teacher. The dialogue might go something like this: Me: "Why am I impatient?" Wise Person: "You may be afraid." Me: "But afraid of what?" Wise Person: "Maybe it's that you'll get behind." Me: "I don't feel competitive. Do you think that's it?" Wise Person: "Maybe it's more fear of survival and always being busy." And so on, until you get the advice you need.

What I like about this technique is that it allows you to solve your problem your way. When we're stuck, we are cut off from our own resources to find a solution. Advice from friends, from this book and others, is all well and good. But you know yourself better than anyone else and, for the most part, other people give the advice that works for them, not necessarily for you. This method, by asking you to consider what someone you respect might say, helps you follow your heart to the answer that is just right for you.

KEEP YOUR BLOOD SUGAR

LEVEL UP

Our nervous system isn't just a fiction, it's part of
our physical body, and our soul exists in space
and is inside us, like teeth in our mouth.

Boris Pasternak

I was driving on a freeway in unfamiliar territory in Southern California with my then mate. "I'm hungry," I declared. "I need to eat something." He pulled off the freeway, searching. We seemed to be trapped in tract housing land. No restaurants in sight. Time passed; I got hungrier and hungrier. Still nothing. I started whining about not finding anything. Finally he spied a Safeway. "Let's try that," he said calmly. I walked into the grocery store, aimlessly wandered the aisles. "There's nothing to eat," I wailed, and stormed out.

All the while I was acting like a lunatic, there was a part of me, my still-reasonable self, observing my behavior and thinking to myself: What is going on? It felt as if I had been hijacked by an alien.

It was only months later that I was diagnosed with low blood sugar, which put the grocery store incident into perspective. If your blood sugar drops too low, you feel irritable, irrational—and impatient. I now recognize the symptoms in others. It's pretty overt: normally reasonable human being suddenly becomes short-tempered, rationality hanging by a thread if not gone altogether.

Parents of small children know this intuitively—kids get cranky when they are hungry. That's why the time just before dinner is often when tempers are the most frayed and patience is the most strained.

I say this to remind you that, while most of the practices of patience are emotional or spiritual, there may be biochemical reasons for your impatience. Maybe you just need to eat.

One way to tune in to this is to pay attention to when you lose your patience. Is it just before mealtimes? Do you seem to regain your equilibrium after eating? You may not feel hungry, even though your blood sugar is low, so it's better to look at the results (I feel more patient after I eat) than the symptoms (I'm hungry). Take note for a week and see if you can discern a pattern. If the answer is yes, for you or someone you love, do what those suffering from low blood sugar do: keep high-protein snacks close at hand. Cheese sticks, nuts, the whites of hard-boiled eggs, or plain nonfat yogurt are all good options.

Keeping up your blood sugar is an easy way to make sure you are giving yourself biochemical help in keeping your emotional equilibrium. It's not fancy, but it sure is effective.

REFRAME THE SITUATION

You will be pleased to know that the heat in Lucknow has been
really hot! . . . It is good to burn with the heat of God outside
since we don't burn with the heat of God in our hearts.

Mother Teresa,
in a letter from Lucknow

A shoe factory sent two marketing scouts to a region of Africa to
study the prospects for expanding business. One scout sent back a
telegram saying, SITUATION HOPELESS STOP NO ONE WEARS
SHOES. The other wrote back triumphantly, GLORIOUS BUSINESS
OPPORTUNITY STOP THEY HAVE NO SHOES.

This anecdote appears in *The Art of Possibility*, by Rosamund
Stone Zander and Benjamin Zander. They use it to illustrate the
point that we are all interpreting reality all the time, so we might as
well tell ourselves stories of possibility.

My daughter reminded me of the usefulness of this recently in relation to patience. I was cooking dinner. Ana was, as usual, at the kitchen table making something out of paper and Scotch tape. She spent at least twenty minutes on this construction. Suddenly, as she went to set it upright, it collapsed in tatters. Did this five-year-old cry, moan, or complain? No, she simply looked at it and said calmly, "That was not a success."

Out of the mouths of babes.

What Ana was doing was choosing to tell herself a story that allowed her to engage her patience and try again. She could have thought, This stupid paper is no good. Or, I'm such a klutz, that's why I can't do this. Or, I shouldn't even try to do things like this. Those thoughts and others like them would have led to frustration, annoyance, giving up.

But by declaring it "not a success," with the implication that the next time she might meet with success, she was able to engage her creativity and motivation to seek a better solution. And that's what she did, running to my desk for cardboard that would make her construction more sturdy, and beginning again.

Ana did this without knowing what she was doing, but we adults can do it on purpose. Psychologists call it reframing—and it is one of the most powerful tools we have to overcome feelings of despair, inadequacy, or irritation, and engage our endurance and resourcefulness. It requires asking yourself one simple question: How else could I look at this that would increase the possibility of a good outcome and/or greater peace of mind?

When I first met my husband, he was thirty-seven and had never been in a relationship that lasted longer than nine months. He spent many years alone, but he never stopped patiently waiting for love. I once asked him how he did that and here's what he said: "Every time a relationship would end, I would say to myself, Well, I guess I still have something to learn before I can be in a long-term relationship." That's reframing. Rather than blaming himself, the other person, or fate, he saw the situation as part of a learning process and therefore could keep his patience until true love arrived.

How can you reframe the patience testers in your life? The next time your blood begins to boil, ask yourself how else you could look at the situation. For instance, I have a friend who proclaims that he relishes the chance to be in traffic because it gives him uninterrupted time to think that he doesn't otherwise get. What you're looking for is an interpretation that offers possibility instead of panic, hope instead of hysteria. Your payoff will be a huge jump in your ability to engage resourcefully with life when it doesn't appear to be going your way.

FIND SOMETHING ELSE TO DO

A great preservative against angry and mutinous thoughts, and all
impatience and quarreling, is to have some great business and interest
in your mind, which, like a sponge shall suck up your attention
and keep you from brooding over what displeases you.

Joseph Rickaby

Ana wanted me to help her do something or other. I was busy
making dinner. "Just a minute," I said. "A minute," she moaned,
"a minute is *such* a long time." "Well," I replied, sounding just
like my mother, "think about something else and the time will go
faster."

Remember the old adage "A watched pot will never boil"? It's
true, whether you are a five-year-old waiting a minute, or a forty-
year-old waiting some unknown amount of time. The more we focus on the fact that we are waiting, the slower the time will go.
That's why, often, the best patience practice we can employ is to do

or think of something else. Preferably, as Joseph Rickaby points out in the above quote, something that is interesting to us.

Doing something else is more than just a distraction device, although it definitely functions that way. When we're in a situation that requires patience (and therefore is out of our control), and we put our attention toward something else, we remind ourselves that not all of our life is out of control. Somewhere we still can take charge; we're not completely at the whim of someone or something else.

When I worked with clients during a time when I was waiting on pins and needles for a buyer for my business, it helped me no end. The more I was effective with them, the more I reminded myself that no matter what happened to my business, I could take care of myself and my family. When Ana distracted herself while waiting for me to come help her by pulling out some crayons and paper, she was proving to herself that she was not completely reliant on me for her happiness. She could entertain herself.

Take a moment right now to think about a situation that is requiring your patience. What could you do right now to gain a measure of control or pleasure in another arena of your life? Waiting for potentially scary test results or to get a call back about a date? Instead of brooding, can you think of something fun or interesting to do in the meantime? How about bringing a magazine when you have to stand in line at the DMV or mentally plan dinner in traffic?

To have patience doesn't mean to dwell endlessly on that which confounds us. It is perfectly all right to put our mind toward something else. Indeed, one anonymous pundit is convinced that patience itself is nothing more than "the art of finding something else to do."

PRACTICE WITH AGING PARENTS

AND OTHER ELDERS

To know how to grow old is the masterwork
of wisdom, and one of the most difficult
chapters in the great art of living.

Henri-Frédéric Amiel

My friend Michelle is turning sixty this year. Her mother, ever more frail, is ninety-seven. For the past twenty-five years, Michelle has increasingly cared for her mother, visiting for weeks at a time, putting her life on hold for her mother's health crises, suspending travel and work, eventually moving across the country to be close. In all those years, her mother has never thanked her for the sacrifices Michelle has made. But Michelle never wavers from her commitment to help her mother have a dignified end of life.

Michelle is no saint. Often she loses her patience, particularly with her mother's inability to comprehend that she's old and can't, for instance, just flip her mattress by herself (which resulted in six months in bed with a strained back). Michelle gets frustrated, annoyed, even angry. But then she forgives her mother and herself and continues on.

In many ways, dealing with aging parents requires the kind of patience that raising children calls for: caring for the person's basic needs because they can't, having steadfast vigilance so they don't injure themselves, constantly being at someone's beck and call, repeating the same information over and over because they can't retain it.

The difference between youth and old age, however, is that as a caretaker of a young person, you can see progress; you're putting in all this effort so that one day your young fledgling can soar on his or her own. With the elderly, we must find other motivations: perhaps because they cared for us or because we want to make the end of their life as pleasant as possible. Each of us has to find our own reasons.

In her diary, *An Interrupted Life*, Etty Hillesum writes of her frustrations in dealing with her parents and what's required to do it well. "What's needed here is not a small act of love. It is something more fundamental and important and difficult. To love your parents deep inside. To forgive them for all the trouble they have given you by their very existence: by tying you down, by adding the burden of their own complicated lives to your own."

At any given moment, however, when our patience is being

tried, such lofty sentiments may not prove useful. What is most helpful at those times is to look at *why* our patience is thin.

Here's how Etty came to understand this: "It really has nothing to do with my father. That is, not with his person, his most loveable, pathetic, dear person, but with something in myself."

When Michelle looked at her situation this way, here's what she discovered: "When I'm with my mother, I see that old age brings vulnerability, and that I will be like that one day. What if I need the kind of help she had to have? What if I suffer so much I couldn't be pleasant? I lose my patience with her because I want her to be the courageous mother of my youth so I don't have to feel afraid of getting old myself.

"That realization helped a lot. So did being compassionate for my own vulnerability, my fear of aging. Every time I'm with her, I say to myself, Yes, you are afraid, yes you are vulnerable. And the more I do that for myself, the more patience I have with her."

You can do it too. Ask yourself, What am I afraid of? the next time you find yourself short-tempered with an elder. The more you attend to your fears, the more patience you summon when you need it.

RESPOND FROM YOUR HEART

How far you go in life depends on your being tender with
the young, compassionate with the aged, sympathetic with the
striving, and tolerant of the weak and the strong—because
someday you will have been all of these.

George Washington Carver

In *One Day My Soul Just Opened Up*, empowerment specialist Iyanla Vanzant writes about a powerful experience with patience. "I was rushing around the house trying to get somewhere I should have been, looking for pantyhose while putting on eyeliner, ironing my blouse while brushing my teeth. It's amazing the number of things you can do when you are late."

The phone rang. It was her son, calling from prison. He'd bitten another inmate in a fight over a comic book and was calling for help. Her first reaction was, "This telephone call was interfering with my plans!" Her son rambled on, frustrated. She could think only of how very, very late to her luncheon she was going to be. Finally he said plaintively, "I'm really not ready to come home yet, am I?"

Suddenly she realized: This is my son. Calling from prison for my help. And I'm worrying about missing a luncheon?

"With all the love and patience I could muster at the moment, I responded, 'Son of mine, you don't have to get an A on life's tests; you only have to pass. You took the time to call rather than stay in the middle of a brawl. If you ask me, I think you are doing just fine.'"

As Iyanla Vanzant discovered, when it comes to being patient with others, the very best thing we can do is engage our compassion. Most of us are doing the best we can, and when we remember that, our hearts open and patience floods in. When we respond from our intellect, we can be very judgmental: she should be like this, he shouldn't be like that. But when we open our hearts, we remember that each of us is an unfinished work of art, a work in progress in the process of becoming.

The fifteenth-century Christian writer Thomas à Kempis noted this in his famous work, *The Imitation of Christ,* when he wrote, "Strive to be patient in bearing the defects of others. You yourself have many also, and they have to be put up with by them. If you are not yourself such as you would wish to be, how could you expect to find another according to your liking?"

It's easy to say we should be compassionate. It's another thing to do it when someone's acting badly toward you. So a great way to put compassion into practice is to step back from the situation and ask yourself three questions my colleague Dawna Markova came up with: (1) If I look at the situation from the other person's perspective, what might he or she be experiencing right now? (2) How would someone I respect put these facts into a different interpretation? (3) If someone I respect did what this person did, would I be feeling differently? If so, how?

These questions help us open our hearts. That's what Iyanla did on the phone with her son. She had a glimpse of what her son was experiencing and her empathy kicked in.

Patience and compassion work in unison to support and build on one another. The more patience we have, the more sensitive and responsive to other people's feelings we will be capable of being. And the more we respond with our hearts instead of our heads, the more we tap into the pool of patience that resides in the center of us all.

TELL YOURSELF YOU HAVE ALL
THE TIME YOU NEED

Life is so short, we should all move more slowly.

Thich Nhat Hanh

I stumbled onto this idea by accident years ago. I was hurrying to do something or other on a deadline and encountered a roadblock—a computer crash, I believe. Just before I felt my impatience rising, I heard myself saying internally, I don't have time for this. As soon as I thought those words, my physical agitation rose, my heart beat faster, my breathing constricted. But there was a little part of my brain, the witness self, that noticed what had just happened. And that witness began to notice that every time I became impatient, it would start by my saying to myself, I don't have time for this. Each time, that thought would trigger the same reaction: fluster and fear.

I hated those panicked feelings. So one day, on a lark because I figured I had nothing to lose, I decided to tell myself that I had all the time I needed. I had all the time I needed to do a project regardless of how many times I was interrupted or the computer froze. I had all the time I needed to get somewhere even if I was stuck in traffic. I had all the time I needed to cook dinner even if we had to be out the door by 7 P.M.

Lo and behold, it worked like a charm. Mostly, I found out, I *did* have the time I needed. It worked so well that it seemed almost magical, as though time expanded or contracted based on my attitude toward it. On a few occasions, I did run out of time, but I still accomplished more than if I had frightened myself with the time scarcity line.

I began to realize that scaring ourselves with not having enough time dramatically diminishes our efficiency and ability to perform. The truth is, the more we stay composed under pressure, the more we are actually able to do because we're using our neocortex, the reasoning, rational part of our mind to help us. With reason, not panic, we may be able to figure out how to unjam the computer, juggle the babysitter's schedule, get to the meeting on time. It's a matter of staying calm rather than flipping out.

Using this self-talk method, I got so much done and was so

graceful under pressure that people in my office began to ask me what my secret was. I shared my strategy and other folks began to use it. It worked just as well for them.

The trick, we discovered, is remembering to do it. Some people put the line on a sticky note and pasted it on their computers. For me, what works best is to stop every time I hear myself saying, I don't have time for this, and replace it with, I have all the time I need.

Experiment yourself. Notice for a week what happens if you tell yourself you have enough time. Is your life saner, happier? More productive? If it works, great! You've just found a way to do more and feel less stressed.

DO A RISK ANALYSIS

When some misfortune threatens, consider seriously and
deliberately what is the very worst that could possibly happen.
Having looked at this possible misfortune in the face,
give yourself sound reasons for thinking that after all
it would be no such terrible disaster.

Bertrand Russell

My friend Annette is one of the most even-tempered people I
know. I've watched her in many different settings, both social and
business, and her serenity is seemingly boundless. It's all the more
remarkable because she has a serious kidney disease, which requires
daily dialysis. Somehow she manages that and the rest of her life
with graceful aplomb. What is the secret to her success? I asked her
one day.

"Well," she explained, "when I find myself beginning to lose my
cool, when the pressure is on, I ask myself, What's the worst possible thing that could happen if I took my time getting through this?

Or if it's something out of my control, like a traffic jam, I ask, What's the worst possible thing that could happen if I am late? Or if the plumber doesn't deliver on his promise to come today to fix the toilet? The answer almost always is, Not much. So what if I'm ten minutes late or that I have to find someone else to fix my toilet? I figure the problems that might get created are nothing compared to the aggravation I'd feel if I allowed myself to get all worked up about it."

A wise woman, that Annette. Her patience method is very straightforward; she does what in business is called a risk analysis: taking a calculated look at what the risks are and whether she could survive them. What she usually discovers is the same thing that you or I would if we did it, that most likely the risk is minimal. The problem is that under stress we get all worked up and feel as though we are in a life-or-death situation.

Even in danger, a risk analysis can be useful. Twenty-four-year-old Ellen MacArthur loves to sail. Recently, this young Englishwoman entered the Vendée Globe, a solo race around the world, against some of the most experienced sailors on the planet. No one expected her to finish.

Alone, she narrowly missed a row of five icebergs. Both her batten and daggerboard broke, necessitating dangerous repairs. ("It's a pretty horrible feeling when you hear the boat breaking up beneath you," she reported in her diary about the daggerboard incident.)

Just twelve hundred miles from the finish line, a rod holding her mast up broke and her boat was nearly crippled for good.

With every challenge, Ellen carefully assessed the risks, calculated her options, and patiently made repairs. The results? She came in second, becoming the youngest person and the fastest woman to ever sail solo around the globe, and only the second person in the world to do it in under one hundred days.

Next time you find yourself all worked up about something, do a risk analysis and notice whether it helps you regain perspective. What *is* the worst thing that could happen? If you find your temperature rising because you are good at catastrophizing, include the following questions: Realistically, what is the likelihood that the worst thing will happen? If the worst did happen, could you survive it—or even do better as a result?

Most likely you will discover that the worst is not likely to occur and even if it did, you would somehow make it. And that awareness can give you the breathing room you need.

KEEP YOUR EYES ON
THE PRIZE

I am extraordinarily patient,
provided I get my own way in the end.

Margaret Thatcher

In his memoir *Nothing Is Impossible*, Christopher Reeve writes of his determination to stand again after a fall from a horse in 1995 left him paralyzed from the shoulders down. Not possible, he was told by medical experts, the spinal cord cannot regenerate; he was lucky to just be alive. But the former Superman set a goal for himself: to stand on his fiftieth birthday in 2002 and toast those who had made it possible for him to do so.

Christopher Reeve did not stand up for a toast on his birthday. But he can sit on his own and he did move his arms and legs—six years after his spinal cord was supposedly irrevocably severed, proof that the cord has regenerated a little. And he is able to feel light touches and pin pricks, again a sign of spinal cord recovery.

He accomplished these feats through an incredibly aggressive daily exercise program that required, among other things, massive patience from him and those who assisted him. Patience to do the same grueling exercises over and over, seemingly with no results.

While he did not reach his target, I believe the fact that he had a goal made patience—and the progress he did make—possible. Because he had something to work toward that really mattered to him, he could endure all the physical suffering that was required. He kept his eyes on the prize.

You don't have to be a superhero to do this. As a result of various home remodeling snafus, my friend Karen ended up living in her house for six months without a bathroom. I asked her how she kept her patience. "I just kept remembering my goal, which was to have a beautiful bathroom that I could enjoy for the rest of my life. Every time I would begin to lose it, I would remember the outcome I was aiming for and my patience would kick in again."

This technique works well with people too. As Margaret Thatcher reminds us in the opening quote, it is precisely our determination to get what we want that gives us the patience we need to work skillfully with others. If we are not steadfast in our wanting, we can easily give up or blow up. When we are committed to what we want, we have the capacity to put up with the situation because we know in the end it will turn out the way we desire.

This determination is a mighty force. In a very real way, we are pulled into the future by the strength of our wanting and the power of our patience. That's because, as Robert Fritz points out in *The Path of Least Resistance*, what we want, if it arises from a state of passion and creativity, doesn't change. It is a stable state, which makes it a powerful magnet for energy to move toward. We don't know how, we don't know when—that's where patience and faith come in—but if we hold our heart's desire strongly enough, we are likely to achieve it.

As a boy, Ted Williams, the last major league baseball player to hit over .400 in a season, had one goal: "to have people say, 'There goes Ted Williams, the greatest hitter who ever lived.' " Shortly before his death, he was nominated to baseball's All-Century Team. As he came onto the field, the announcer's voice rang out: "There goes Ted Williams, the greatest hitter who has ever lived."

The next time you find yourself being thwarted in what you want, see if you can use the energy of your frustration to fuel what you want even more strongly. Say to yourself, The more this person or thing gets in my way, the more I will remember what I truly want. Engaging our determination in this way is more than a trick to pass time. It actually increases the odds that our dreams will become reality.

UNDERWHELM YOURSELF

I'm late, I'm late, for a very important date. No time
to say "Hello," "Goodbye." I'm late, I'm late, I'm late.

*the White Rabbit in Lewis Carroll's
"Alice's Adventures in Wonderland"*

Sheila and Ted are married with two young children. Ted is a computer programmer who works an hour away from home. Sheila is a nurse who works evenings so that she can be home in the mornings because her son's kindergarten is in the afternoon. Ted leaves for work early so that he can come home at three o'clock when the kids get out of school. Ted and Sheila communicate by notes and don't see each other during waking hours except on weekends.

"It all works fine, until it doesn't," Sheila confided to me recently. "School holidays, a kid sick, and the whole thing blows up. I'm always on edge, worrying when it will fall apart next." Sheila also complains about being constantly impatient with her kids: "They call me the drill sergeant," she lamented. Is it any wonder? There's no breathing room in their lives.

While their schedule may be more convoluted than most, Sheila and Ted are not alone in juggling a great deal. We all do. A single mom wrote to me recently that despite her best efforts to be kind and patient, "I find myself practically pushing old ladies aside to get to the subway on time. And I fume at soccer practice when a coach doesn't end the practice exactly on schedule, because I have to race across town to get another kid."

Recently I came across a statistic that said that the average American couple is working one hundred hours more a year now than in 1980. One hundred more hours! (And we in the United States work something like four hundred hours more yearly than our European counterparts, who certainly do seem to be more laid back and having more fun.) No wonder we're all strung out and short-tempered. We're doing too much and we're not taking enough time off.

And despite the simplicity movement, we can't stop. We couldn't stop in the nineties because we were in the midst of an economic boom that we needed to try to get our piece of. Now we can't stop because times are tough and we have to prove our worth or lose our hard-to-get job. Or we have to work full-time at finding a job. Then there are our household duties, the kids' gymnastics lessons, school and church functions. And what about the personal growth we're committed to? Working out? Flossing our teeth? I'm tired just typing the list. No wonder we get impatient with any obstacles in our path.

That's why one of the ways to have more patience is to, in the words of author Dawna Markova, underwhelm ourselves whenever and wherever possible. Do ten things instead of twenty; take a nap instead of going out; leave for the meeting a half hour early so you don't have to stress over getting there.

The most patient people I know are those who have plenty of time in their lives for whatever life throws at them—a broken tooth, a flat tire, a sick child. Their lives have enough elasticity in them to accommodate such curveballs and so they can respond with patience and compassion.

Take a moment right now to think about how you could begin to underwhelm yourself. Think you can't eliminate anything from your list? Try looking at it as choices you've been making, choices that you can change if you want to.

Sheila saw that she'd been choosing to solve the problem on her own without looking around for other resources. She and Ted ended up inviting his mother to live with them. Now they always have a backup caretaker and driver and Ted, Sheila, and their kids are much more patient—and happy.

How can you reclaim your life?

ASK YOURSELF: IS THIS THING

STILL FLYING?

We are all dangling in mid-process between what already happened
(which is just a memory) and what might happen (which is only an idea).
Now is the only time anything happens. When we are
awake in our lives we know what's happening.

Sylvia Boorstein

My husband is a rambling storyteller. Now, I've lived with him for
ten years so you would think I would be used to it by now. Recently
he began a story with the words, "I want to tell you something because it could have bad consequences for this business deal you've
been putting together." Before he could finish his sentence, my
heart started racing, I went into panic mode and began yelling,
"Just tell me right this second! Just tell me right now!" (So much for
the practice of patience!) My outburst got him so flustered that it
took him a full five minutes to get the story out.

When I later looked at my reaction and thought about what causes me to lose my patience in general, it often has to do with some fear. Something happens and I become convinced that it will lead to a bad end if it is not dealt with RIGHT NOW!

That's why I was so attracted to the story I read about former Apollo astronaut Alan Bean. Bean, like most astronauts, had previously been a test pilot and test pilots are trained to ask one question when something goes wrong in the air: "Is this thing still flying?" It's a way of helping the pilot mentally evaluate how serious a problem is rather than panicking so that he or she can calmly come up with a solution.

That training came in handy, Bean relates, when he was in the Apollo 12 capsule. As the spaceship took off, it was struck by lightning. Suddenly every warning light on the instrument panel flashed, and the astronauts on board felt under tremendous pressure to DO SOMETHING. But then, said Bean, he remembered the question. The spacecraft was not only still flying, but it was still headed in the right direction—to the moon. So he decided not to abort the mission, but patiently dealt with each warning light one by one until all functions were restored. And yes, they successfully made it to the moon.

Chances are the things that cause you and me to lose patience are not so immediately life-threatening as being in a spaceship struck by lightning. That should make it even more possible for us to stop and ask, "Is this thing still flying?" In other words, am I truly in a life-or-death situation or do I have time to calmly evaluate my options?

Whether it took my husband one minute or four to tell me his story, I was in no immediate danger. And of course, from a composed place, I could be much better prepared to deal with whatever information he had to convey even if it were terrible news.

Next time you find yourself out of patience with someone or some situation, try the flying test. It's a great way to restore some much-needed perspective.

5.

TWENTY SIMPLE
PATIENCE BOOSTERS

In addition to the practices suggested in Section 4, here are easy things you can do on the spot when you are looking to increase your patience.

1. If you've got a big project you're working on, choose to notice what you've done rather than what you've got left to do. The "glass half full" approach increases patience because it taps into our sense of positivism. As one man wrote about building a boat, "I don't think about how long it will take. Instead I notice how far I've come."

2. At your tolerance limit with someone at work or home? Try a vigorous walk or jog. You'll burn off the stress hormones that have accumulated in your system and will be more able to reengage your patience when you return.

3. The old advice to count to ten before speaking in a heated situation really can work. It gives you a chance to remember what really matters to you—blowing off steam or finding an effective solution. If ten doesn't work, try twenty. Keep counting!

4. Seek practical solutions to the things that irritate you about your mate rather than nag. Get a refrigerator with an automatic ice cube maker if you go nuts about your sweetie always forgetting to fill the ice cube trays; get the toothpaste that comes in a pump if you see red at the sight of the cap left off. Many such simple solutions exist if we look for them.

5. Put a small pebble in your pocket. When you start to feel irritation rise, move the pebble from one pocket to the other, which will help interrupt the anger cycle and give you a chance to regroup.

6. Standing in line, take yourself on a mental vacation. Visualize the most peaceful place you can think of. See, feel, and hear yourself there. Bring to mind the feelings that such a place evokes in you. Rather than focusing on how long you have to wait, relish this chance to take a little daydream to Tahiti or the Alps.

7. Kids, parents, spouse making your blood boil? Remember what legacy you want to leave in the world. That your father says on his

deathbed that you were so kind? That your son thanks you for being a patient teacher to him? Take a minute now to think of what you would want to be remembered for after you are gone and bring it to mind in times of relationship trials.

8. Start a patience movement. Thank others for being patient when you've been the one fumbling for the right change and holding everyone up. It will defuse their tension and yours, and perhaps encourage others to do the same.

9. When you have to wait a long time for something to come to fruition—a big project, for instance—celebrate small milestones along the way. Ten pages done? Take yourself to lunch. When we reward ourselves for what we've accomplished, we give ourselves the resilience to press on.

10. No time to go on retreat? Use waiting in line to practice walking meditation. Feel your feet on the floor. Carefully pick up one foot, noticing how it feels to do that. Place it carefully down and with awareness, then lift and place the other foot. See how long you can focus on lifting and placing. When you find your mind wandering, gently return it to noticing your walking. You will not only be calmer while waiting, but will be building your patience muscle.

11. Waiting impatiently for your computer to boot up? Do the rag doll, which relaxes back and neck muscles. Push away from the desk, sit on the edge of your chair with your knees and feet about twelve inches apart. Put your head between your knees, allowing your hands to rest on the floor between your feet. Breathe and allow your irritation and tension to flow out of your body into the floor.

12. Try the red-light meditation. Use a red light, ringing phone, or other frustration to notice three breaths. Simply notice how your breath goes in and comes out, without trying to change it.

13. Try mindfulness in chores. When wiping the kitchen table, for instance, really notice what you are doing. Feel your arm as it moves back and forth; enjoy the shine you are creating. It will take no longer than doing it mindlessly and by bringing yourself fully to the enjoyment of the experience, you have more patience for it.

14. Cut down or swear off caffeine. Caffeine is a stimulant that can cause jitteriness and yes, irritability, the inability to take life in stride. According to one study, more than half of Americans consume more than the recommended amount of two hundred milligrams per day. (The average cup of coffee contains one hundred milligrams.) When I found myself drinking as much as a quart a day of iced tea, I switched to decaf. Yes, I had a blinding headache

for a day, but it was worth the price for the increase in calmness and patience.

15. Tuning out when someone's talking? Think about a time in your life when you needed someone to be patient with you and they were. When you remember the healing power of patience in your life, you'll have more with others.

16. Would I rather be right or effective? That's a great question to hold in your mind when you're in a conflict with someone. Use it as often as you need to keep your goal—and your patience—front and center.

17. Find an inspirational quote (this book has plenty) that you can put on your computer, on your bathroom mirror, in your car. When you find patience slipping, read it for an immediate booster shot.

18. Ask for help. Lots of times we are impatient because we are overloaded. There's no prize at the end of your life for doing too much, particularly if you do it in a frazzled state.

19. Try laughing at yourself or your situation. Christopher Reeve writes eloquently about how joking helps him. When asked how he was doing in the early stages of his paralysis, he replied, "Well, my

throat's a little scratchy, I have an itch on my nose, and my finger-nails need cutting. Oh—and I'm paralyzed."

20. Testy at the office? Go online to www.unwind.com for soothing pictures and music, as well as relaxation exercises that you can do at your desk. Or give yourself a laugh at www.theonion.com.

6.

ABOVE ALL, BE MERCIFUL

WITH YOURSELF

Have patience with all things, but chiefly have patience
with yourself . . . every day begin the task anew.

St. Francis de Sales

I once came upon a quote that said, "A patient man is one who can
put up with himself." Over time, I've come to better understand the
wisdom of those words and the ones above by St. Francis. For, in
the cultivation of patience, we are really being called on to love ourselves in all our brokenness and beauty, when we stumble as well as
soar.

The longer I've pondered patience, the more I've come to see that impatience is actually a symptom of perfectionism. If we expect ourselves and others to be perfect, if we expect subways and elevators and voice-mail systems to be flawless, then we will lose our patience every time some imperfection shows up: lost luggage, blown timetables, rude waiters, fussy in-laws, cranky kids. Conversely, the more we see life as messy and unpredictable, and people as bumbling through life the best they can, the more patience we bring to the circumstances and people in our lives.

But we can't do that unless we start with patience for ourselves, by treating ourselves with compassion for, and curiosity about, our foibles and failings. If we expect perfection from ourselves, we're rigid, inflexible, judgmental. Any mistake is unacceptable so we push it away and pretend it never happened. We don't learn from our errors and are therefore condemned to repeat them. If, on the other hand, we treat ourselves in a tender, gentle manner as a loving mother would treat her newborn child, it's possible to acknowledge our mistakes and make wiser choices in the future.

As we cultivate this heart habit called patience, we deserve our own mercy. "Mercy" is an old-fashioned word; you don't hear it much these days. "Mercy," writes French philosopher André Comte-Sponville, "is the virtue of forgiveness. . . . mercy is that path which accommodates even those who fail to reach its end."

I love this word because among its meanings is this: compassionate treatment of those in distress. When we show ourselves mercy, we cradle our distress, our irritation and anger. We hold it close, we allow it to touch and thereby transform us. We melt our rigid insistence that we must be perfect. Even if we haven't lived up to our own standards, we love and care for ourselves anyway, just as we are—in our woundedness, with our strength. And the more love and mercy we shower on ourselves, the more patience we'll have to flow over to the rest of the imperfect people who populate this less than perfect world.

Love and patience are two intertwining strands, like the DNA that is the foundation of human life. With love, we can be patient—with ourselves, with others, with life itself. With patience, we can love—ourselves, other people, and the mysterious, awe-inspiring journey of life. Each strand informs and supports the other, each inevitably teaches about the other.

One of the greatest inspirational writers of the nineteenth century was a man named Henry Drummond who wrote a best-selling little book entiled *The Greatest Thing in the World*. In it, he said, "The world is not a playground; it is a schoolroom. Life is not a holiday but an education. And the one eternal question for us all is *how better can we love*."

May your patience give you the capacity to meet that grand challenge and may your love—for yourself as well as others—lead you to grow your patience until it shines brightly in the world for the benefit of all.

My Thanks

Overflowing thank-yous to Dawna Markova, who supports me in everything and is extremely generous in allowing me to share what I've learned with and through her. Her perspective that patience is a verb was particularly helpful, as well as many suggestions on how to practice. She is the wisest person I know in terms of what supports real change in human beings.

Boundless appreciation to my husband, Donald McIlraith, for graciously allowing me to reveal so much of his life and our relationship, and for being one of my greatest patience teachers. A bow of loving respect and gratitude to Ana Li, my five-year-old, who is so wise in patience and so many other regards. Thanks for putting up patiently with Mama working so many weekends.

Thanks to Bonnie Clark, Kathy Corbett, Tigest Scott, and especially Don for loving care of Ana so I could work on this book on a very tight deadline. Appreciations to Rick Weiss, Mary Beth Sammons, Barb Parmet, and Susie Kohl for stories, concepts, constructive criticism, and keeping me from repeating myself. Many thanks to Robin Rankin for metaphor and quiz support, and to her and the rest of my colleagues at Professional Thinking Partners—Dawna Markova, Andy Bryner, Dave Peck, and Angie McArthur—who covered for me as the deadline approached.

Thanks to my editor, Kris Puopolo, who strongly believed in the need for a book on patience and placed it in a larger social context than I had been seeing. Her suggestions blew my story that big New York publishers don't have great developmental editors. Also to agent extraordinaire Debra Goldstein, who waited patiently for me to be free to work with her and delivered on her word to the letter.

Finally, a deep bow of gratitude to the writers of all spiritual persuasions whose teachings inform the pages of this book, and to those clients and friends who've shared their journeys of emotional and spiritual growth with me. To preserve the latter's privacy, I have changed their names and the details of their stories, but I hope the spirit of what they have taught me and what we've learned together remains.

Bibliography

Armstrong, Lance. *It's Not About the Bike*. New York: Berkley Publishing Group, 2000.

Beck, Martha. *Expecting Adam*. New York: Berkley Publishing Group, 2000.

Boorstein, Sylvia. *Pay Attention, For Goodness' Sake*. New York: Ballantine Books, 2002.

———. *Road Sage*. Audiotape. Boulder, Colo.: Sounds True, 1999.

Brussell, Eugene E., ed. *Dictionary of Quotable Definitions*. Englewood Cliffs, N.J.: Prentice-Hall, Inc., 1970.

Cohen, Darlene. *Finding a Joyful Life in the Heart of Pain*. Boston: Shambhala, 2000.

Comte-Sponville, André. *A Small Treatise on the Great Virtues.* New York: Henry Holt and Company, 1996.

Dalai Lama. *An Open Heart.* Boston: Little, Brown and Company, 2001.

———. *Healing Anger: The Power of Patience from a Buddhist Perspective.* Ithaca, N.Y.: Snow Lion Publications, 1997.

———. *How to Practice.* New York: Pocket Books, 2002.

Dyer, Wayne. *There's a Spiritual Solution to Every Problem.* New York: HarperCollins, 2001.

Fadiman, James, and Robert Frager. *Essential Sufism.* San Francisco: HarperSanFrancisco, 1997.

Frank, Jan. *A Graceful Waiting: When There's Nothing More That You Can Do, God's Deepest Work Has Just Begun.* Ann Arbor, Mich.: Servant Publications, 1996.

Fritz, Robert. *The Path of Least Resistance.* New York: Fawcett, 1989.

Gallwey, W. Timothy. *The Inner Game of Work.* New York: Random House, 1999.

Gleick, James. *Faster: The Acceleration of Just About Everything.* New York: Vintage, 1999.

Goleman, Daniel. *Emotional Intelligence.* New York: Bantam Books, 1995.

Hanh, Thich Nhat. *Anger*. New York: Riverhead Books, 2001.

Harned, David Baily. *Patience: How We Wait Upon the World*. Boston: Cowley Publications, 1997.

Hillesum, Etty. *Etty Hillesum: An Interrupted Life and Letters from Westerbork*. New York: Henry Holt and Company, 1996.

Jennings, Jason, and Laurence Haughton. *It's Not the Big That Eat the Small . . . It's the Fast That Eat the Slow*. New York: HarperBusiness, 2000.

Kidd, Sue Monk. *When the Heart Waits*. San Francisco: HarperSanFrancisco, 1990.

Kyi, Aung San Suu. *Letters from Burma*. New York: Penguin Books, 1995.

LeFan, Michael. *Patience, My Foot! Learning God's Patience Through Life's Difficulties*. Joplin, Mo.: College Press, 1993.

Le Joly, Edward, and Jaya Chaliha, eds. *Reaching Out in Love: Stories Told by Mother Teresa*. New York: Continuum, 2000.

Mack, Gary, with David Casstevens. *Mind Gym*. Chicago: Contemporary, 2001.

Mandela, Nelson. *Long Walk to Freedom*. Boston: Little, Brown and Company, 1994.

Markova, Dawna. *I Will Not Die an Unlived Life*. Berkeley, Calif.: Conari Press, 2001.

McClelland, Carol. *Seasons of Change*. Berkeley, Calif.: Conari Press, 1998.

Mello, Anthony de. *Awareness*. New York: Doubleday, 1990.

Moon, Janell. *Stirring the Waters*. Boston: Tuttle Publishing, 2001.

Peale, Norman Vincent. *Words That Inspired Him*. New York: Inspirational Press, 1994.

Reeve, Christopher. *Nothing Is Impossible*. New York: Random House, 2002.

Remen, Rachel Naomi. *Kitchen Table Wisdom*. New York: Riverhead, 1997.

Sapolsky, Robert M. *Why Zebras Don't Get Ulcers: An Updated Guide to Stress, Stress-Related Diseases, and Coping*. New York: W. H. Freeman and Company, 1998.

Sarriugarte, Tracy, and Peggy Rowe Ward. *Making Friends with Time*. Santa Barbara, Calif.: PBJ Productions, 1999.

Segal, Jeanne, Ph.D. *Raising Your Emotional Intelligence*. New York: Henry Holt and Company, 1997.

Shenk, David. *The End of Patience: Cautionary Notes on the Information Revolution*. Bloomington: Indiana University Press, 1999.

Sherman, James. *Patience Pays Off*. Golden Valley, Minn.: Pathway Books, 1987.

Tenner, Edward. *Why Things Bite Back: Technology and the Revenge of Unintended Consequences*. New York: Vintage, 1996.

Tolle, Eckhart. *The Power of Now*. Novato, Calif.: New World Library, 1999.

Ullathorne, William. *Patience and Humility*. Manchester, N.H.: Sophia Institute Press, 1998.

Van Kleeck, Gail. *How You See Anything Is How You See Everything*. Kansas City: Andrews McMeel Publishing, 1999.

Vanzant, Iyanla. *One Day My Soul Just Opened Up*. New York: Simon & Schuster, 1998.

White, Rosalyn, ed. *The Magic of Patience: A Jataka Tale*. Berkeley, Calif.: Dharma Publishing, 1989.

Wilde, Jerry, and Polly Wilde. *Teaching Children Patience Without Losing Yours*. Richmond, Ind.: LGR Publishing, 1999.

Zander, Rosamund Stone, and Benjamin Zander. *The Art of Possibility*. New York: Penguin Books, 2000.